RETHINKING

LAW

made possible by a generous grant from
THE WILLIAM AND FLORA HEWLETT FOUNDATION

Rethinking Law is *Boston Review* Forum 22 (47.2)

"Make Progressive Politics Constitutional Again" is adapted from *The Anti-Oligarchy Constitution: Reconstructing the Economic Foundations of American Democracy* by Joseph Fishkin and William E. Forbath, published by Harvard University Press. Copyright © 2022 by the President and Fellows of Harvard College. Used by permission. All rights reserved.

"The Imperial Roots of the Democracy of Opportunity" by Aziz Rana is adapted from the Law and Political Economy blog.

"What Movements Do to Law" by Amna A. Akbar, Sameer Ashar, & Jocelyn Simonson is adapted from the article "Movement Law," published in *Stanford Law Review* 73.4 (April 2021).

To become a member, visit store.bostonreview.net/memberships

For questions about donations and major gifts, contact María Clara Cobo, mariaclara@bostonreview.net

For questions about memberships, call 877-406-2443 or email Customer_Service@bostonreview.info.

Boston Review
PO Box 390568
Cambridge, MA 02139

ISSN: 0734-2306 / ISBN: 978-1-946511-72-0

CONTENTS

ESSAYS

EDITORS' NOTE

Deborah Chasman & Joshua Cohen

A CONSERVATIVE SUPREME COURT is poised to roll back many progressive achievements of the late twentieth century, from affirmative action to abortion. Income and wealth inequality are a continuing—and growing—disgrace. Structural barriers to democracy impede popular accountability, from the Senate to the Electoral College, and the orderly transfer of power is itself under threat. All the while, the U.S. criminal justice system—with its powerful racial inflection—remains the most punitive such system on our burning planet.

Legal scholars Joseph Fishkin and William E. Forbath argue that a progressive response to these challenges demands a decisive break from postwar liberal legalism. After the New Deal, they argue, liberals sought to cordon off both law and the economy from democratic politics. For a brief period, judicial supremacy—with the Supreme Court settling the meaning of the Constitution—looked like a good bet, yielding greater civic inclusion and deference for progressive legislation. In the end, though, it was a poisoned pawn, as judges won unprecedented power to constrain legislative initiatives and threaten the affirmative state. The alternative, Fishkin and Forbath contend, is to recover a lost vision of progressive politics—what they call the *democracy-of-opportunity* tradition. That tradition marries a substantive, political-economic vision—a racially inclusive, anti-oligarchic Constitution—with a democratic conception of the public, not the judiciary, as the ultimate arbiter of constitutional meaning. Respondents explore the prospects of this ambitious proposal and wonder whether it is ambitious enough to address our most serious challenges.

Other essays in this special issue—designed with the help and guidance of *Boston Review* contributing editor Amy Kapczynski— further reflect on the meaning of law beyond the Constitution and the courts. Some look to social movements, from queer liberation to reproductive and racial justice, for lessons about social transformation and the limits of legal demands. Others examine contested legal concepts, including human rights and Martin Luther King, Jr.'s conception of "unjust laws." Together they offer a nuanced picture of the relationship between law and politics. As Paul Gowder notes in his contribution, our moment of legal precarity might best be served by what critical race theorist Mari Matsuda once called "multiple consciousness." In a deeply unequal society, the law can certainly impede progress, but it also remains an essential resource in building a more just world.

MAKE PROGRESSIVE POLITICS CONSTITUTIONAL AGAIN

Joseph Fishkin &
William E. Forbath

TWO YEARS of a devastating pandemic have exposed deep cracks in the U.S. political and economic order. After decades of economic policies that hollowed out the middle class, shocking numbers of Americans lacked the economic means to withstand COVID-19's disruptive force. But the pandemic also demonstrated that economic policy is not set in stone. For a brief moment, before collapsing back into familiar patterns of polarization and obstruction, the federal government stepped in with the money to rescue vast numbers of Americans from economic ruin.

The Democrats are, for now, about two Senate votes shy of enacting a series of major reforms that would address climate change, voting rights, and the outsize political and economic power of the rich. But even assuming that Democrats manage to enact such measures

—overcoming our system's many antidemocratic veto points, such as the Senate itself—the toughest challenge is still to come. The looming risk is that all such reforms may be unraveled by the Supreme Court. The Court has made the Constitution a weapon for selectively striking down legislation the justices disfavor. They are highly likely to wield it against laws that aim to repair economic or political inequality.

The Court can do this with near-total impunity because many Americans accept the idea that the Supreme Court is the only institution with any role in saying what the Constitution means. Congress and other elected leaders, at best, can fill in the few blanks that the courts have left open. Rather than contesting the Court's power to make highly questionable judgments about the meaning of the Constitution, most liberals today defend the Court's authority. Their top complaint about the current Court is that it doesn't have sufficient respect for its own precedents, which today's majority is fast overturning as it lurches further right.

Mounting an effective challenge to our conservative juristocracy requires understanding how we got here. It is not just that the right out-organized the left. On the contrary, liberals have contributed to conservatives' success by imagining constitutional law as an autonomous domain, separate from politics. Liberals have likewise imagined that most questions about how to regulate the economy are separate from politics, best left to technocrats. These two ideas have different backstories, but both were at the center of a mainstream liberal consensus that emerged after World War II. For postwar liberals, constitutional law was best left to the lawyers, economic questions to the economists. These two key moves sought to depoliticize vast domains that had previously been central to progressive politics. Together they tend to limit the role of the people and the representatives they elect.

Conservatives never accepted either of these moves. They have a substantive vision of a political and economic order they believe the Constitution requires, and that vision translates easily into arguments in court—arguments against redistribution, regulation, and democratic power. Inspired by their forebears a century ago in the Lochner era, when conservative courts routinely struck down progressive reforms for violating protections for property and contract, today's conservatives have methodically installed movement judges who reliably advance those goals. And they are succeeding. Witness the litigation over the Affordable Care Act (ACA). Although the law narrowly survived, conservatives outside and inside the courts embraced novel arguments that Congress had transgressed constitutional limits on its powers. Liberals disagreed, offering arguments that the ACA was *permissible*. But they never made the argument their progressive forebears might have made: that something like the ACA is *required* to meet our constitutional obligations.

In response to the right's decisive politicization of the courts, some liberals and progressives have proposed judicial reforms aimed at restoring an imagined past of judicial nonpartisanship. But that golden age is a myth. Constitutional confrontations over rival visions of our political and economic future are inevitable; courts are *always* engaged in such contests. The problem is not that the judiciary has a vision of constitutional political economy. The problem is that

that vision has strayed much too far from the views of the elected branches and the people.

Bringing the Court back in line will be a challenge. Fortunately we have precedents to draw from. For the first two-thirds of U.S. history, generations of reformers—from Jacksonian Democrats to Reconstruction Republicans to New Deal Democrats—made arguments in what we call the *democracy-of-opportunity* tradition. These reformers argued that the Constitution not only permitted but compelled legislatures to protect U.S. democracy in the face of oligarchy and (later) racial exclusion. The Constitution, in this tradition, not only permits, but compels, the elected branches to ensure the broad distribution of power and opportunity that are essential to a democratic society.

Reformers made these arguments in the teeth of hostile courts determined to impose court-made doctrines to shield elites from democratic encroachment. But the elected branches could and often did challenge the Court's interpretation of the Constitution, especially about the trajectory of the nation's political economy—the political decisions that shape the distribution of wealth and power through our laws and institutions.

This vision is worth retrieving today. Some progressives will think this is a misguided, even dangerous, proposal. If constitutional law is the domain of the courts, and courts are dominated by conservatives, why should we risk "re-constitutionalizing" our claims about political economy? Why, in short, should progressives make our politics constitutional again? The fear—that any talk of the Constitution cedes power to courts—is understandable.

Fishkin & Forbath

But the opposite is true. Not speaking about the Constitution in politics cedes power to courts. By making claims on the Constitution, we show that all branches of government, and the people themselves, have the authority and duty to debate what our constitutional principles require.

There is no future for the liberal idea (never adopted by conservatives) of a sharp separation between constitutional arguments in court and political arguments outside the courts. The border between the two is too thin and porous. Arguments move across it both ways, with profound effects. Declarations by courts shape the terms of public debate and move the horizons of political possibility; arguments in politics shape arguments in court. We are all responsible for participating in debates about the meaning of the Constitution, and we ought to recognize the power of this shared commitment. In the long run, it can help us build a more egalitarian and democratic society than some of our elites, on and off the Court, would accept.

What might such efforts look like? Today's conservatives wield their anti-redistributive vision of constitutional politics primarily as a sword for attacking and striking down legislation. In the progressive constitutional politics we envision, rooted in the democracy-of-opportunity tradition, the Constitution in court functions largely as a shield: to demonstrate to judges, and the rest of us, why egalitarian, democratic legislation should be upheld against constitutional attack.

We see at least three key battles. First, it is time for progressives to reclaim the First Amendment, contesting the way it has been weaponized as a tool to thwart egalitarian legislation in campaign finance and labor law. Second, we must reforge the link between racial justice and political economy, widening the constitutional lens through which we see questions of race beyond antidiscrimination law and voting rights, to include substantive issues of mass incarceration, health care, public investment, job creation, and wealth inequality. Third, we must bring political economy back into view in areas where liberals retreated from politics and ceded power to economists, such as in antitrust, monetary policy, and corporate law.

To challenge the constitutional claims of hostile courts, progressives must first persuade Americans that certain progressive ideas are deeply rooted in U.S. traditions of constitutional argument. In pursuing these ideas, we are not transgressing constitutional boundaries but rebuilding the economic and political foundations of democracy.

Repairing the First Amendment

THE FIRST AMENDMENT was not always what right-wing courts today have made it. When it rose to prominence in the first half of the twentieth century, the First Amendment was invoked to protect not only dissenting, unpopular speech, but also workers' freedoms of collective action, especially picketing and strikes. In the hands of lawmakers and labor leaders—and briefly even in the courts—it worked to diminish the inequalities of power between capital and labor, helping to preserve sources of countervailing power against oligarchy. But in the hands of today's right-wing Supreme Court, the First Amendment has been weaponized as a tool for dismantling egalitarian forms of self-government. Our current court reads the First

Amendment in ways that undermine not only the labor unions that workers democratically elect, but also the campaign finance regimes that our elected leaders enact in an effort to preserve democratic self-rule. It has become a pro-oligarchy amendment.

This is a neat trick. It works the same way every time. In place of democracy, the modern court sees only a bureaucratic state. Instead of people attempting to work together to govern ourselves, the modern court sees, in every First Amendment case, simply a fight between two actors: a lone individual plaintiff whose "speech claims" are pitted against the regulatory goals of a hostile government. If we look beyond the lone plaintiff and the state, we see something else: the numerous ordinary people whose power, in politics and in economic life, depends on collective self-government as a bulwark against oligarchy.

Consider how First Amendment jurisprudence has recently played out in campaign finance reform. In a run of cases beginning in 2008, a narrow conservative majority eviscerated a series of campaign finance laws because they aimed, as the majority of justices put it, to "level the playing field" or "equalize" the power of different actors in the political sphere. One law was a "millionaire's amendment" that allowed federal congressional candidates to raise extra money when faced with a rich, self-funded opponent; a similar Arizona law gave extra public matching funds to candidates who faced especially well-financed opposition. As Elena Kagan noted (in dissent), such a law "does not restrict any person's ability to speak," but instead, by its express terms, "creates more speech." Still, such laws do indirectly disincentivize wealthy candidates and independent groups from spending their money in political ways. In other words, the laws intervene in our political economy in a way that inhibits the conversion of economic power into political power. The point was to inhibit oligarchy, and that is why this conservative Court struck them down.

A similar pattern of argument prevailed in 2010, when the same narrow majority held in *Citizens United v. FEC* that Congress could not bar corporations from spending their treasuries on political advertising. U.S. law had long drawn a line between corporations themselves, whose political activities were restricted, and political action committees (PACs), which are often affiliated with a corporation but are legally separate. (PACs are funded by corporations' executives and supporters—who are citizens, as entitled as anyone else to participate in politics.) But in *Citizens United*, the majority swept that distinction away. If corporations themselves want to spend money to speak about politics, Anthony Kennedy held, "the Government" must not "impose restrictions on certain disfavored speakers."

These arguments make clear that conservatives hold a vision of constitutional political economy in which economic power is freely convertible into political power—and in which what most people might call "corruption" is reconceived as ordinary politics, subject to constitutional protection.

In his *Citizens United* dissent, John Paul Stevens argued that "our lawmakers have a compelling constitutional basis, if not also a democratic duty, to take measures designed to guard against the potentially deleterious effects of corporate spending." His reference to "democratic duty" is highly unusual today. It evokes a lost world of democratic lawmaking, one that acknowledged that legislators have a constitutional duty to build the countervailing political power of the democratic majority against the wealthy few.

How should lawmakers wield this "compelling constitutional basis" to respond to *Citizens United*? Both state legislatures and Congress could give large unconditional sums of campaign money to any serious candidate for office. They could create public small-donor matching funds, as in New York City, where the city matches small contributions (under about $250) from residents at an 8:1 ratio. The higher the ratio, the closer the system comes to democratizing campaign finance, by giving ordinary voters the clout to shape who runs for office and who wins. H.R. 1, the democracy reform bill that was passed by the House of Representatives in 2021, but was filibustered in the Senate, would create a nationwide small-donor match system for congressional elections.

Lawmakers can also alter the political economy of running for office—and improve the prospects of candidates and movements with poor and working-class constituencies—by making it less expensive to run a campaign. Existing Federal Communications Commission rules require broadcasters to offer certain modestly favorable terms for candidates' political advertising. Congress could go much further, adapting this rule to apply to Internet platform advertising and requiring broadcasters and Internet platforms to provide a floor of very inexpensive, or even free, advertising to political candidates. These ideas are realistic legislative actions that are consistent with even the current Court's judge-made doctrinal Constitution. But, if enacted, they will face constitutional challenges anyway, with novel extensions of First Amendment doctrine offered as reasons to strike them down. To explain to the people—and not just to courts—why those challenges should fail, progressives should meet these arguments head on. There is not only constitutional power, but a constitutional duty, to preserve a democratic political economy.

The weaponized First Amendment has similarly upended labor law, turning its constitutional stakes upside down. Before World War II, Franklin D. Roosevelt and his congressional allies had argued that constitutional democracy and political self-rule could not exist alongside industrial "despotism." Recalling the Jacksonians' core anti-oligarchy insight, that the laboring "many" needed mass organizations with the clout to counter the wealthy "few," New Dealers declared that their labor law reforms would come to the republic's rescue by finally "incorporat[ing] the industrial workers in the polity of the United States" as a "check upon the power of 'Big Business.'"

When law students learn about the New Deal and its defense of the industrial union today, they focus on the expansion of national power through the Commerce Clause. That was part of the story. But at the time, the era's leading scholar of the Supreme Court, Edward Corwin, saw things quite differently. He saw a constitutional "revolution" taking place—not about the commerce power, but about the constitutional meaning of freedom. Safeguarding workers' collective freedoms against private employers' coercion—and guaranteeing "the economic security of the common man" through social insurance—were now "affirmative" governmental obligations.

Unsurprisingly, for decades the remnants of this vision have been squarely in the crosshairs of conservative politicians and judges. Starting with the counterrevolution of the late 1940s, the "right to work" movement has waged an ongoing campaign of legislation and litigation—funded and supported by corporate executives and employers' associations, as well as by wealthy anti-union ideological activists—to destroy the New Deal vision of labor as a source of countervailing social and political power against oligarchy.

The conservatives aimed to redefine unions as entirely private collective bargainers, acting exclusively on behalf of current members in their negotiations with a single employer. This campaign's first great success, the Taft–Hartley Act of 1947, prohibited so-called secondary boycotts, in which workers act in solidarity to aid fellow workers in a dispute with a different employer. Taft–Hartley also prohibited "closed shops" (where an employer agrees to make union membership a condition of employment). From then on, there would be nonunion workers in unionized workplaces. But would the nonunion workers have an unfettered right to free ride on everything that the union had bargained for? Taft–Hartley allowed states to say yes, through "right to work" laws, which some (mostly southern) states promptly enacted. Elsewhere unions often negotiated for "agency fees," in which those who didn't join the union would nonetheless pay a fee, reducing the free-riding problem. This raised a new issue: workers who disagreed with a union's politics, and refused to join for that reason, might now be supporting some of its political speech.

In *Abood v. Detroit Board of Education* (1977), the Court saw a First Amendment problem with this arrangement and drew a careful line. A union could charge agency fees for the costs of collective bargaining, contract administration, and grievances (all of which it was required by law to undertake on behalf of all the workers at the workplace, whether union members or not). But it could not use agency fees for political speech. Later, however, the Court retreated from this position and came to view union activity as essentially private and economic, not public and political. That was how the Court justified upholding Taft–Hartley's various limitations on activity such as boycotts and picketing against First Amendment challenges.

This compromise could not survive the Court's recent rightward shift. In 2018, in *Janus v. AFSCME*, the Court brought the hammer down, overturning *Abood* and holding that, at least for public employers (the private-employer case is still to come), the First Amendment requires that every state become a "right to work" state. Unions must fully allow nonmembers to free ride, charging them no fees for the services the unions must provide them.

As today's liberal justices stare down a far bolder and more sweeping anti-labor intervention, insights about labor as a countervailing power are nowhere to be found. For lawyers focused on the action inside the Court, making such arguments in the face of conservative majorities might seem pointless. But this concern misses the role constitutional arguments play in public debate. They not only shape litigation but also send signals to the political branches and the people about what cases like *Janus* are really about—not speech, but constitutional political economy. Rebuilding a powerful progressive movement with a central place for organized labor requires forging a new understanding of the constitutional necessity of countervailing power—an understanding that will have to begin life outside the courts, but ultimately will reverberate both inside and out.

There is a path forward. Democrats committed to labor law reform have gained power within the party. Not since Harry Truman vetoed Taft–Hartley in 1947 (a veto later overridden by the conservative Dixiecrat/Republican coalition) has the White House spoken about workers' right to organize the way President Joe Biden speaks about it. Although Democrats do not yet have the votes in the Senate, the House recently passed a sweeping labor law reform bill, the Protecting the Right to Organize Act (PRO Act), which aims to repeal crucial elements of Taft–Hartley and boost efforts to organize unions. Among other things, the PRO Act would expand the definition of work to ensure that organized workers in today's fragmented workplace—from fast food franchise workers to "contracted" Uber and Lyft drivers, to home health care workers—can bargain with the companies who benefit from their work. The PRO Act would repeal some of the most crippling restrictions on the rights to strike and boycott, such as the ban on so-called secondary actions, which blocks workers who have some organized economic clout from aiding workers who don't. As the House Education and Labor Committee puts it, the act would enable "unions to exercise these basic First Amendment rights." It is very encouraging that this view—that the Taft–Hartley prohibitions violate basic constitutional rights—is once more gaining strength in Congress.

Enacting transformative labor law reform will involve fierce and protracted battles, not only in the Senate, but in courts (where challenges are inevitable), in workplaces, and in the public sphere. Getting there will require both Democratic majorities committed to such change and considerable labor organizing and action on the ground. As in the 1930s, workers will need to exercise their rights to organize, strike, and act in solidarity in contexts where this is now illegal, in the face of judicial injunctions, fines, and jail time.

Conservatives will attack any new legislative protections for workers with novel legal arguments. They will find First Amendment arguments against efforts to restrain employers' anti-union activity. They will make federalism arguments that Congress lacks the power to upend states' traditional common law and police-power authority to limit forms of labor solidarity. Progressives will need more than the old liberal response that Congress has broad power under the Commerce Power to regulate the national economy, and that Congress has exercised that power to promote labor peace. Both in court and outside of it, and in legislative bodies from city councils up to Congress, progressives should work to show their fellow citizens that rebuilding labor is a constitutional necessity.

Race, Class, and the Reach of Public Law

AS LONG AS Americans have fought over the meaning of the Constitution, they have fought about race. But these days the scope of questions of race and the Constitution has narrowed. We all can see the constitutional dimension of affirmative action or race and policing. But we have lost sight of an older idea: that racial justice is bound up with political economy.

Reformers during Reconstruction understood that without major changes to the South's political economy—government provision of education, federal power to enforce voting rights, the redistribution of land from the deposed oligarchs to the freedmen who worked it—generations of servitude and oligarchy would be followed by generations of other forms of hierarchy and dependence, rather than full citizenship and democracy.

They were right. It is not possible to unravel the layers of racial hierarchy and oppression at the heart of U.S. political and economic life without substantially renovating U.S. political economy. Mainstream liberals lost sight of this idea in the mid-twentieth century, but it has remained central to the radical tradition of Black thought that includes W. E. B. Du Bois, Pauli Murray, Bayard Rustin, Martin Luther King, Jr., Coretta Scott King, the Movement for Black Lives, and William Barber's Poor People's Campaign.

Opponents of racial inclusion have also long understood the connection between racial inclusion and political economy. They have not trained their fire exclusively on race-conscious programs like affirmative action. Instead they have consistently chosen lines of constitutional attack that reduce the potential of public law to intervene in our political economy in ways that might promote a broader distribution of economic or political power. They have also pressed the interventions of public law downward, away from the federal government and toward the states. This gives southern, white political elite more power to block interventions that might benefit Black people. Finally, they have worked to carve out constitutional domains where private law norms of contract and property trump public policy interventions such as antidiscrimination law.

Consider the Affordable Care Act. The most important piece of the legislation was a large expansion of Medicaid to provide health care—and with it, some basic measure of economic security and independence—for Americans with income below 133 percent of the poverty level. Yet in his 2012 majority opinion in *NFIB v. Sebelius* that kneecapped this part of the act, Chief Justice John Roberts complained that Medicaid "is no longer a program to care for the neediest among us, but rather an element of a comprehensive national plan to provide universal health insurance coverage." In political-economy terms, the policy's ambition to provide a kind of universal social insurance was indeed as dramatic as Roberts described. Roberts's decision allowed states to opt out of the Medicaid expansion—to keep the old program in place, creating a large class of working poor people suddenly ineligible for any form of subsidized health insurance—a wild outcome that Congress never imagined.

To reach this surprising result, Roberts had to build new constitutional doctrine. Forcing states to accept a broad and universal program for the poor and the working class, or else lose the narrower and stingier program they had before, was "coercion," Roberts held, a "gun to the head"—and therefore unconstitutional, according to an account of the relationship between the federal government and the states that elevates the constitutional entitlements of states over those of citizens. Roberts's opinion caused well over 2 million Americans to become uninsured. But this was no random set of Americans. About nine out of ten of the people deprived of health insurance live within the boundaries of the former Confederacy, and a vastly disproportionate number of them are Black. This fight might seem very distant from the hot-button, constitutional conflicts over race. And yet it is all about race: built on centuries of laws and policies of racial exclusion, the political economy of social insurance has a profound racial dimension.

In a parallel move the following year, in *Shelby County v. Holder*, Roberts destroyed Section 5 of the Voting Rights Act, which required heightened federal oversight for places with a history of excluding racial minorities from voting. The ruling predictably unleashed a new politics of voter disenfranchisement in the formerly covered jurisdictions. Roberts held that Section 5's differentiation among states was unconstitutional: it violated a kind of quasi–equal protection principle that applied to states, not people. This "equal sovereignty" principle, as Roberts called it, is not part of the Constitution's text, any more than the anti-coercion principle that limits federal spending powers in *Sebelius*. They both sound as if they rest on general ideas about the nature of our federalism. But in fact, even as they loosely evoke antebellum southern constitutional ideas, these principles were recently custom-built for targeted interventions in constitutional political economy.

In response to the Court's cynical enabling of a state-level politics of disenfranchisement, Congress must enact new, clear, universal statutory schemes protecting voting rights—and must then be prepared for a protracted fight with this Court. The Medicaid expansion is also a statutory provision with constitutional weight. Congress still can, and should, undo the Court's constitutional intervention by enacting statutory reforms that take the question of basic health insurance coverage for working-class people of all races out of the hands of state governments that are too wrapped up in the racial politics of anti-redistribution to protect the core economic interests of their own constituents.

Conservative justices are meanwhile carving out a growing statutory and constitutional exception to civil rights laws. They are rapidly building a jurisprudence that reads the Religious Freedom Restoration Act (RFRA) and the First Amendment together to give religious individuals, groups, organizations, and even corporations the power to opt out of a widening range of generally applicable public laws, including antidiscrimination laws. To the extent that these changes are reversable by statute, Congress should reverse them. But a constitutional battle is inevitable.

In a society marked by vast racial inequalities in wealth, education, employment, and capital, there is much more to do. The Movement for Black Lives and the Poor People's Campaign have proposed programs of public investment, job creation, and community economic development that resemble a twenty-first-century Freedom Budget. The movement for reparations for Black Americans has gathered steam, and policies for addressing wealth inequality—such as baby bonds, wealth taxes, and homeownership-related asset-building—are now being framed by prominent lawmakers in expressly racial terms. As these proposals gain political support, they too are certain to draw opposition framed in constitutional terms, inside and outside the courts.

For example, if Congress enacts a wealth tax, it should anticipate a constitutional confrontation. Old ideas about constitutional political economy that limited the reach of the federal taxing power will be dusted off and revived. Congress should anticipate such a confrontation by devising alternative taxes on accumulated wealth—perhaps a more robust estate or inheritance tax—that would kick in immediately if a wealth tax were struck down. Other strategies for taxing concentrated wealth might include reshaping corporate taxes to more effectively tax wealth or rents. The precise contours of the new policy matter less than the politics of enacting it: whether Congress chooses a wealth tax or a less direct route to the same goal, its policy must be accompanied by a strategy for contesting hostile judges' visions of constitutional political economy.

Antitrust, Ownership, and Democracy

THE LIBERALS of the late twentieth century believed that many economic questions were best left to technocratic experts. This was a mistake, and one measure of its magnitude is the extent to which, since the 1970s, the U.S. economy has become increasingly monopolistic, with most sectors dominated by a small number of firms. Entrepreneurial activity is now at an all-time low. Central to this transformation of the economy have been profound changes in antitrust policy, corporate law, tax and monetary policy, lobbying regulations, and many other areas of public law. When liberals learned to think of these important spheres of constitutional political economy as technocratic policy problems, they forgot hard-won lessons about their constitutional stakes.

Those stakes were very clear to Americans working in the democracy-of-opportunity tradition throughout the nineteenth and early twentieth centuries, including those in the antimonopoly movement in the Gilded Age, Reconstruction-era Republicans such as Senator John Sherman (namesake of the foundational Sherman Act), and Louis Brandeis in the Progressive Era. From their point of view, the purpose of antitrust was to preserve a democratic republican constitutional order, one in which no single economic actor would be sufficiently powerful to crush competition or direct the power of the state to its own ends.

But in the 1980s, with the help of the Reagan Justice Department, Robert Bork and his allies in what came to be called the Chicago School convinced judges and regulators to discard this entire tradition of antitrust thought. They read into the Sherman Act a vision of economic well-being that prioritized the interests of Americans as consumers, not as producers, and certainly not as citizens. Regulators began to excuse monopolies' predatory behavior toward competitors as long as they kept consumer prices low. The predictable rise of monopoly has been a significant factor in the sharp decrease in the share of economic output that is paid out to workers—and to the meteoric rise in inequality overall.

Today a full-fledged movement is emerging to advocate a return to a more Brandeisian conception of antitrust law. Antitrust is a mechanism—not the only one, but a very important one—to prevent the concentration of too much economic and political power in too few hands. As Zephyr Teachout and Lina Khan have argued, "Excessive corporate size tends to hurt democratic self-government because it enables a handful of actors to purchase disproportionate political power and to subject citizens to systems of private governance

that become less accountable the bigger and fewer the corporations."
These neo-Brandeisians are making a claim that Brandeis would have
found obvious, but that today requires argument: antitrust law is
"constitutional" in nature.

An antitrust law focused on oligarchy would be far less tolerant of
mergers, and far more likely to break up monopolies and oligopolies,
than the antitrust law of recent decades. It would be considerably less
confident in government's long-run ability to impose behavioral conditions on companies (a common substitute today for blocking mergers
or breaking up monopolies). It would curb oligopolistic practices in
industries where a few firms have outsize power, as well as practices
such as the noncompete agreements that many employers demand
from workers by contract. It would curb the power of agribusiness
giants to govern and control the actions of small producers. But this
is not simply about making antitrust law more aggressive. An antitrust law in the democracy-of-opportunity tradition would be more
permissive than the law is today when it comes to labor: workers or
small producers banding together look dramatically different, from
an anti-oligarchy perspective, than does a cartel of large firms with
great market power.

Any such effort will certainly be challenged in court. Business
interests will find ways to claim that antitrust regulators are taking
their property, invalidating bargained-for contracts with suppliers or
employees, or exceeding constitutional limits on federal power. The
constitutional arguments will, as ever, take place both inside and
outside the courts, and will cross the membrane separating the two.
But reformers today must not lose sight of the core idea: constitutional

democracy requires an underlying political economy that is democratic rather than oligarchic.

These ideas could also animate a series of changes to U.S. corporate law. Over time, and especially since the 1980s, a relatively pluralistic and contested conception of whose interests corporations must serve has given way to the view that corporations exist exclusively to maximize the returns to their shareholders.

In the early republic, the prevailing view was that corporations were "artificial persons," chartered to serve public purposes and in need of being supervised and held to account by legislatures and courts. The turn toward an exclusive focus on shareholders was not inevitable. Corporate governance could transform it again. Senator Elizabeth Warren, for example, has proposed legislation that would require the largest corporations to obtain federal, rather than state, charters. The terms of the charters would specify that these large corporations must "consider the interests of all corporate stakeholders—including employees, customers, shareholders, and the communities in which the company operates."

Regardless of the specifics, any effort to modify U.S. corporate law in this direction will face constitutional challenge. Some conservative commentators already argue that mandating codetermination would violate the Takings Clause of the Fifth Amendment. Others may argue, for example, that the law violates the First Amendment rights of corporations by giving employees an effective veto over corporate speech.

Both inside and outside the courts, the core argument for codetermination is straightforward: we are choosing to build a regime of corporate governance that is compatible over the long run with democratic government. That was the constitutional argument that Progressives like Brandeis and Herbert Croly put forward. There could be no more "political democracy" in the United States, Brandeis argued, without workers' "participating in the decisions" of their firms as to "how the business shall be run." Today this idea seems distant, but the core insight behind it remains as true as ever: we have choices about how to set up the political economy of the United States, and our choices have implications for our constitutional democracy.

IN THE FACE of massive inequality and a dangerous trend toward oligarchy, progressives today are beginning to reclaim some elements of the democracy-of-opportunity tradition. This essay has only scratched the surface of a few of the areas where that is happening. This nascent revival of anti-oligarchy thinking is more than the sum of its parts. It is not just policy, but constitutional argument. Past generations of progressives understood this; their conservative opponents did too. Indeed, those conservative opponents never stopped understanding it. In preparation for a series of massive confrontations with a far-right court, it is time for progressives to once again mine this rich vein of U.S. constitutional history and constitutional thought.

Our Constitution is the constitution of a republic, not an oligarchy. It can continue to work that way only if we manage to prevent excessive concentrations of political and economic power.

We must disperse political and economic power widely enough to ensure that economic opportunity is broadly shared and racially inclusive. These are not merely constitutionally permissible goals; they are constitutional necessities. Legislators and citizens who hope to reverse the present slide into oligarchy need to recover these arguments and deploy them to help rebuild the democratic foundations of our republic.

Fishkin & Forbath

UP FROM ORIGINALISM
Andrea Scoseria Katz

ALEXIS DE TOCQUEVILLE OBSERVED that in the United States, almost every political debate ends up becoming a legal one. During his visit in 1831, he watched Americans incorporate legal language and ideas "in their daily polemics" and concluded that the spirit of the lawyer "infiltrates all of society." Tocqueville had a point: even today, if you can convince an American that something is legal, it's a short step from there to convincing him that it's good. Conversely, if a policy is presumptively unconstitutional, however wise or helpful it might be, it's out.

Legal philosopher Brian Tamanaha has written about this phenomenon with regard to what he calls the "problematic asymmetry" between left and right discourse about law. The right talks fidelity to the text; the left views constitutional law as a means of achieving desired social ends. (During his confirmation hearing in 2005, for example, Chief Justice John Roberts said he would just "call balls and strikes.") But this rhetorical framing of the left's and right's respective jurisprudential philosophies is of recent vintage, obscuring far more than it shows.

In fact, it was not so long ago that progressives attacked conservatives for "loose construction" that strayed from the text. In 1896, just twenty-four years after the Supreme Court held that "the one pervading purpose" of the Fourteenth Amendment was race equality, it was endorsing "separate but equal" train cars in *Plessy v. Ferguson* and rapidly transforming the Fourteenth Amendment's Due Process Clause into a protective shield for corporations against labor. Between 1886 and 1910, of the 307 Fourteenth Amendment cases that came before the Court, 288 involved corporations seeking "due process" rights of natural persons; 19 dealt with African Americans. "Due process," wrote political scientist Edward Corwin, was "not a legal concept at all." It was instead a roving torpedo judges could use "to sink whatever legislative craft" seemed to them to be "of a piratical tendency."

Public opinion was no kinder. The 1895 *Pollock* decision, which struck down the federal income tax, inspired calls across the country to impeach the justices and abolish judicial review altogether. After the 1936 *United States v. Butler* ruling gutted a New Deal agricultural program, a passerby in Ames, Iowa, discovered six life-sized effigies of the majority opinion justices hanged by the side of a road.

The political axis flipped for a time after World War II, when a Warren Court liberal on criminal procedure, voting rights, and civil rights convinced progressives to make their peace with judicial solutions to political problems. As Joseph Fishkin and William E. Forbath note, "constitutional law was best left to the lawyers, economic questions to the economists." But in winning the battle, progressivism lost the war. Once the Court's composition changed, around the time Warren Burger became chief justice in 1969, the bargain was easily undone. With a friendly ear on the bench, conservative lawyers were eager to jump into the void, armed with a utopian vision of the American way of life under small government, Christian faith, and family, and a novel (albeit thoroughly ahistorical) theory of the fixed original meaning of the Constitution—one that was not living but emphatically "dead, dead, dead." The new "originalist" jurisprudence—at its core, a political project aimed at rolling back progressive judge-made change—quickly gained traction with the conservative elite and had a transformational effect on the courts in the intervening decades.

The stakes of this transformation are apparent in case after case over the last half century. In 1977 the Court saw no problem in defending state bans on Medicaid coverage for abortions with the observation that, "The indigency that may make it difficult—and in some cases, perhaps, impossible—for some women to have abortions is neither created nor in any way affected by" the government's refusal to provide coverage. In 1974 it decided that segregated public schools in Detroit produced by redistricting and white flight were not a problem unless deliberate discriminatory intent could be proven in these developments. (Within a decade and a half of the case, Detroit's public schools were 90 percent Black.) In 2007 the Court gutted a Seattle public school busing program, reasoning that "racial balancing" was "patently unconstitutional," even if done in the interest of promoting diversity.

In contrast to the "originalist" views of this new generation of conservative jurists, Fishkin and Forbath urge us to read the Constitution in a spirit of pragmatism, animated by values that promote our nation's democratic health, and to forge a new, popular constitutionalism based on an egalitarian vision of political and economic order under our Constitution. I thoroughly endorse this project. But so long as a conservative Supreme Court with textualist leanings remains the final arbiter of questions of constitutionality, this will be an uphill battle. To succeed, progressives must be prepared to dismantle the powerful fictions of a "fixed meaning" to the Constitution and of a politically neutral Supreme Court that simply calls balls and strikes. While a new program of constitutional thought is a necessity for advancing a vision of an anti-oligarchic, egalitarian Constitution, it must be paired with conscious efforts to dismantle a jurisprudential sleight of hand that claims, first, that constitutional meaning is fixed, and second, that only judges are capable of understanding it.

Thankfully, our nation's constitutional beginnings support this project. As Tom Ginsburg has put it, our Framers were "committed empiricists." They approached the task of regime-building with what David A. Strauss has characterized, in a different context, as a spirit of humility, fully aware that the text would have flaws and gaps that others down the road would need to fill. (Alexander Hamilton, for example, admitted in an echo of Hume that "no human genius, however comprehensive," could write a constitution that couldn't do with improvements down the line.) A jurisprudence hostile to learning from our own mistakes is nowhere required by our founding document, and it probably would have been disapproved by our own founders. In fact, in the years after the Founding, our nation was knit together—and the Court's own powers of constitutional interpretation established—by none other than "loose constructionist" Chief Justice John Marshall.

Will this convince the dyed-in-the-wool originalist that a progressive constitutionalism is desirable or necessary? Probably not. But these scholars, part of a tightknit ideological movement that hardly speaks for the ordinary American, should not be the audience for a democratic movement. (They are, however, worthy foes for progressive constitutionalists aiming to tear down originalism's privileged status as method.) When Fishkin and Forbath call for reclaiming the First Amendment to make it safe for labor again, reforging the link between racial justice and political economy, and bringing concerns of economic justice back into fields like antitrust, monetary policy, and corporate law, I read them as saying that the choice to make the law blind to justice—i.e., shutting our eyes to the realities of money, history, race, and power—is just that: a choice.

The political upshot is that movement conservatism will not lose its rhetorical advantage unless Americans come around to the idea that we can decouple the law from value-blind formalism. Fishkin and Forbath's most fundamental insight might be this: at bottom, there are thick and ineliminably political disputes about how to interpret what our Constitution says and requires. And if interpretation is inescapably political in this way—if it always involves more than calling balls and strikes—then the courts must not be the sole vehicle for it: both popular movements and popular representation have a primary role to play.

Today, we must reverse postwar liberalism's retreat to Great Society bureaucracy. We have to repoliticize the act of interpretation itself—not by trying to "capture" or "tame" the Court, but by looking beyond it, by winning battles in the arena of popular politics. We need a vision, grounded in the Constitution, of a more just United States. We can and should opt to build a new popular constitutionalism, but we should be well-prepared for a difficult battle ahead.

THE IMPERIAL ROOTS OF THE DEMOCRACY OF OPPORTUNITY
Aziz Rana

IN THEIR ESSAY for this forum, and in the book from which it is adapted, Joseph Fishkin and William E. Forbath have provided a pathbreaking intervention in constitutional history and politics, one that will fundamentally reshape how scholars imagine the relationship between the Constitution and the economy. For decades there has been a taken-for-granted left-liberal framework for thinking about the connection between the Constitution and the economy. Its roots stretch back to Oliver Wendell Holmes, Jr.'s dissent to the Supreme Court's infamous 1905 decision in *Lochner v. United States*, which struck down New York state maximum hour laws in the baking industry. Holmes defended the legality of such labor protections by saying that the Constitution embodied no "particular economic theory." As a result, Holmes thought, it should be the political branches' responsibility to decide how to regulate the market or to determine distributive outcomes.

Fishkin and Forbath rightly note that the liberal embrace of this outlook has had disastrous consequences. The desire to cabin off the economy from the Constitution has left liberal legal voices ill-equipped to address the depredations of U.S. capitalism. It has meant that scholars and lawyers have largely ignored the structural features of the constitutional order that have promoted the business right's assault on social democracy. It has also meant that while business conservatives have developed a sophisticated judicial analysis contending that the Constitution requires their preferred distributive outcome, left-liberal lawyers have by and large failed to offer an alternative legal vision of what constitutes a democratic political economy. Fishkin and Forbath address this profound lacuna by looking to a democracy-of-opportunity tradition, one critical of oligarchy and committed to socioeconomic equality and broad-ranging inclusion.

All of this is to be applauded. What I want to do here is explore one of the thorniest issues connected to the democracy-of-opportunity tradition: the persistent political link in historical practice between U.S. imperial power and internal economic equality. My comments are less a critique of Fishkin and Forbath's argument and more an attempt to think through why the tradition has remained historically incomplete and only partially fulfilled. They certainly highlight how the "tragedy of American political and constitutional development" entails the longstanding wedding of "democratic and egalitarian aspirations to the racist causes" of slavery and Indigenous dispossession, not to mention gender subordination. As Fishkin and Forbath are well aware, the problem with U.S. constitutional development has been more than a failure to live up to inclusive ideals. The actual historical high tides for the domestic experience of democracy of opportunity have very clearly occurred during periods of territorial and global expansionism.

One can appreciate this link by exploring the law and politics of the mid-nineteenth and mid-twentieth centuries. With respect to the long Jacksonian era, Thomas Piketty notes in *Capital in the Twenty-First Century* (2014) that throughout the 1800s—indeed even during the Gilded Age—wealth inequality in the United States was "markedly lower than in Europe." Piketty does not provide a proper explanation for why, but the answer is fairly evident. Throughout the century, the dominant collective project was the imperial one of "settling" Indigenous land—expropriating territory and demographically replacing Native with white communities. This project provided easy access to property, cut against oligarchic tendencies, and facilitated small-scale white producerist democracy. White settler society did have its persistent class inequalities. But it was empire that fed the cultural embrace of Jacksonian white egalitarianism and made the democracy-of-opportunity tradition real for countless white laborers. In this way, the tradition was inextricably a settler imperial one.

There are striking resonances too with the mid-twentieth century. In his history of labor in the 1970s, *Stayin' Alive* (2011), Jefferson Cowie quotes the son of a white steelworker, who recalled the dramatic material improvements his family enjoyed following World War II: "If what we lived through in the 1950s was not liberation . . . then liberation never happens in real human lives." The background context for this boom was the war and its aftereffects, in particular the transformation of the United States from one among various global players to the dominant economic force in the world. With

European powers decimated, the United States essentially became the hegemonic actor. Its currency emerged as the global reserve currency, and through the carrot of development assistance and the stick of military intervention and violent coups, it reconstructed foreign states in its image, in the process opening markets for U.S. goods. Such economic and military dominance was the international underpinning for the domestic promotion of white middle-class prosperity.

This historical connection between empire and the experience of democracy of opportunity carries serious political and constitutional implications. Politically, perhaps the greatest challenge facing any effort to recover the tradition for the present is that it has historically been strongest through the flexing of external power. In other words, while there is a clear record of what amounts to imperial social democracy in the United States, a practical history of linking anti-imperialism with genuine economic transformation is far sparser.

This fact also underscores a key reason why those high tides were so politically partial. In the 1800s, even the more inclusive versions of settler democracy—the agenda Reconstruction Republicans pursued after the Civil War, for instance—by and large rested on an overarching project of settler colonization. White Republicans at their most expansive still saw civil rights for Black people as perfectly compatible with frontier expansion and Native absorption—the elimination of Indigenous nations as independent political communities sharing the same territorial landmass. There was limited space in political life for a truly anti-imperial vision that would have combined Black freedom and Indigenous self-determination.

As legal historian Mark Graber has demonstrated, this phenomenon eventually had effects on white Republican interest in Black voting rights in the South. The continuous party push to open western land to settlement meant that Republicans less committed to Black equality found an alternative mechanism for ensuring that the party maintained its national dominance. Where those like Thaddeus Stevens may have wanted to create a multiracial political coalition built around the southern Black vote, others could imagine the party enjoying permanent majority status through midwestern Republican constituents settling new states and electing reliably Republican politicians to the House, the Senate, and the presidency. In short, empire offered what Graber calls a "westward alternative" to an inclusive democracy of opportunity.

As for the twentieth century, it was not a coincidence that the post–World War II settlement treated jobs, pensions, and health insurance as private entitlements for workers to negotiate from employers rather than as universal public goods. The terms of U.S. global primacy dramatically elevated the position and wealth of U.S. business, in ways that made corporate interests seemingly coterminous with the public interest. The result was precisely that white workers could embrace a settlement as "liberation" that nonetheless gave up on actual economic democracy. Over time, as economic conditions changed and U.S. corporations squeezed workers abroad and then at home, what remained of the mid-century achievements largely disappeared. Thus, not unlike the 1800s, it is fair to conclude that

U.S. empire both provided the backdrop for the ultimate postwar framework, but also was partly responsible for why U.S. social democracy fell so short.

There have been constitutional costs as well, with proponents of the democracy-of-opportunity tradition embracing coercive legal regimes. For Jacksonians, the goal of internal white settler democracy justified legal frameworks that gave government actors broad discretion to employ violence in pursuing territorial expansion as well as in organizing the racial management of subordinated communities. During the mid-twentieth century, it was again not an accident that New Dealers and postwar liberals were also the central architects of the national security state. This design went hand in hand with legal doctrines that ensured extensive deference to presidents and to officials when unilaterally applying force overseas or pursuing security crackdowns at home.

None of this is to suggest that one should simply do away with the democracy-of-opportunity tradition. Its political and legal links with empire were complex ideological configurations rather than philosophical requirements. Still, this history is our inheritance, and many of the figures venerated for promoting a more democratic political economy certainly understood their own imperial projects as necessarily and intrinsically joined.

Fishkin and Forbath have provided an essential intellectual and political contribution by placing constitutional arguments from this tradition at the center of our conversations about law and capitalism and in recovering a past emancipatory language. But we must also take the historical record seriously. How can we create political movements that instead wed anti-imperialism and democracy of opportunity, reversing what has been the far more common cultural linkage? Only by severing the ties between domestic economic reforms, nationalist belligerence, and external power projection will the democracy-of-opportunity tradition promote equal and effective freedom for all.

NOT ONLY LOOKING BACKWARD

Mark Tushnet

JOSEPH FISHKIN AND WILLIAM E. FORBATH offer an impressive manifesto for progressives thinking about the Constitution we need now. They look to U.S. historical experience with progressive constitutional change. They offer both a *method* of achieving that change and the *content* the authors argue should be pursued. The method is what some have called "political constitutionalism," in contrast to our current fetishism of judicial constitutionalism; the content is a new political economy.

The manifesto looks to the past for guidance. The authors want to "make progressive politics constitutional *again*." They describe a vision "worth *retrieving*," and they want to "*rebuild* the democratic foundations of our republic." This retrospective language flows from the authors' attempt—completely successful, in my view—to establish that political constitutionalism is part of the repertoire of thinking and development in U.S. constitutional discourse. Indeed, they contend that political constitutionalism pervaded constitutional thinking until the New Deal, after which a "great forgetting" occurred. To retrieve that tradition, then, is to work within our constitutional heritage, not move outside it.

I'm completely on board with the effort to revitalize political constitutionalism in the United States—that is, with their proposed method. The democracy-of-opportunity tradition combines a political economy with a quest for inclusion that is indeed worth retrieving. But it is also essential to recognize that looking to the past has its limits, and that a narrow focus on oligarchy doesn't cover all the problems we face. Here I sketch four items, absent from the history Fishkin and Forbath rely on, that should be in a progressive constitutional manifesto for the twenty-first century.

First and most obvious, I think, is an agenda for the environment, including responses to the effects of past and future climate change. I note that their essay only mentions climate change in passing and doesn't include the words "environment" or even "Green New Deal"—a program that blends a forward-looking concern for the environment with a backward-looking one for workers in today's industries. Exactly which environmental and climate related policies should be part of the agenda of progressive political constitutionalism is not something legal scholarship can resolve, of course—but I'm quite sure that they must be part of any vision of progressive constitutionalism, and that progressives should spend some of our time discussing and developing a range of options.

Second, we certainly need an agenda for structuring and regulating the modern information- and service-based economy. The authors argue for reviving the antitrust tradition to deal with mega-corporations in the information economy, for modifying our understanding of the First Amendment to allow regulatory interventions responding to those corporations' business models, and for restructuring labor law in ways that would allow traditional labor unions to deal with gig employment and more generally the new service economy. All well and good, but I suspect that the political economy of a stable democratic information and service economy will require more creative institutional responses. Unlike workers in traditional industries, gig workers don't regularly congregate; reaching them to promote collective action has already elicited some ingenious organizational techniques, and more will be needed. The concept of a "normal work week" probably has to be modified to take account of new working modes.

Third, the inclusiveness agenda—grounded in the historical experience first with African Americans and then with women, immigrants, and LGBTQ+ persons—must be transformed. The quest for inclusiveness—perhaps extending so far as non-human animals, too—is far from complete, of course, and perhaps never will be. But as Charles Taylor and many others have forcefully argued, inclusion isn't the only goal anymore; recognition is. Policies aimed at recognition might include treating multiculturalism as a constitutionally mandated component of the curriculums in our schools and more generally abandoning the "melting pot" understanding of the United States—as a nation where everyone eventually becomes blended into a uniform culture—for a multicultural one, where we each preserve and extend our distinctive cultures while simultaneously recognizing that we are compatriots of everyone else. Again, more important than any specific policy recommendation is a commitment to conceiving of recognition as a matter of constitutional concern.

Finally, I revert to a historical perspective to note that an important strand in political constitutionalism has always sought reforms of existing institutions: expansion of the franchise, direct election of senators, mechanisms of direct popular governance such as the initiative, referendum, and recall—all were important parts of the Progressive agenda in the early twentieth century. Sometimes these institutional reforms were aimed at overcoming obstacles existing institutions placed in the path to enactment of progressive substantive reforms; sometimes they were sought to deepen democracy itself. What institutional reforms might be part of today's progressive agenda?

Now we are in my wheelhouse, and I can be a bit more expansive. Though their focus on political constitutionalism understandably leads Fishkin and Forbath to forgo substantial discussion of Supreme Court reform, some Court reforms might promote political constitutionalism. I've suggested, for example, enactment of a statute, modeled on Scandinavian constitutional provisions, that would direct the Court to invalidate national statutes only if they were "manifestly inconsistent" with the Constitution. (I feel compelled to add that fleshing out this proposal requires more explanation and justification than I can offer here.) Substituting direct election of the president for the current system using the Electoral College is another reform that ought to be on the table, already with quite substantial popular support.

Beyond that lies a wide range of possible innovations in democratic governance, many of which have been tried on a small scale in the United States and elsewhere. I'll mention my own hobbyhorses, but I'm far more interested in having progressives discuss democracy-enhancing reforms than in insisting that these particular three innovations must be part of the contemporary progressive constitutional agenda.

1) Deliberative polling with law-making effect. The technology of "deliberative polling"— which brings together a diverse group, presents them with detailed information about a policy issue, and lets them hash out their differences to come up with some resolution—is now reasonably mature. So far it has been used mostly to generate advice to legislatures, sometimes to shape agendas for referenda. There's good reason to believe that deliberative polling can generate policy outcomes that are both better substantively and closer to what an informed public would prefer than the ones produced by representative legislatures. Representatives are elected on general party platforms, strike deals across policy areas, and respond to influences from campaign donors and lobbyists. All this can be excluded from a well-designed deliberative poll.

2) Injecting random selection into representative bodies. We trust randomly selected jurors to make decisions with vast personal and financial consequences. Recently scholars have made that case that random selection of legislators—or at least random selection of some legislators—makes sense too. Ordinary people can bring a perspective to important questions of public policy that professional politicians can't, especially because politicians, whatever they come from initially, almost inevitably become part of an elite that stands apart from the people whose lives their decisions affect. Belgium has taken some tentative steps in this direction by creating "deliberative" committees that include randomly selected citizens who sit with elected members to present proposals to regional parliaments.

Tushnet

3) Decentralizing some important questions of public policy. In *Seeing Like a State* (1998), political scientist James C. Scott showed that on some questions, decision-makers at the center simply know less about what policies would promote valuable goals than ordinary people at the periphery. Bureaucrats at the center directed that trees be planted in orderly rows to facilitate record-keeping; people on the ground knew that sustainable forests were disorderly and included scores of different kinds of trees. Having policy made at lower than national levels, even down to our neighborhoods, might often be better for the nation as a whole. Details matter, of course: it's hard to see how an effective system of paying for health care could be organized locally, and exclusionary housing policies famously result from decisions by local homeowners. Saying that decentralization isn't a universally desirable practice, though, isn't to say that it can't be done and used for progressive goals. Here, too, creative progressive thinking about local governance seems to me valuable.

Again, the point is not these three—or indeed any particular—reforms must be part of the progressive constitutional agenda for the coming century. Fishkin and Forbath are quite right in saying that progressives should retrieve the tradition of political constitutionalism they so clearly describe. But as we develop such an agenda, we should think about what distinctive institutional changes will be required in the future in order to promote the reconceived democracy of opportunity.

BEYOND NEOCLASSICAL ANTITRUST

Sanjukta Paul

IN THEIR RECOVERY of the democracy-of-opportunity tradition of constitutional argument, Joseph Fishkin and William E. Forbath make a powerful case in favor of the affirmative governance obligations created by the Constitution, particularly in the arena of economic life. Antitrust law is particularly ripe for this project: it is both central to the authors' anti-oligarchy framework and has been totally remade in the modern era by the style of economic reasoning that, in general terms, they rightly criticize as the natural accompaniment of the hollowing-out of progressive constitutionalism. I offer here two suggestions for sharpening this aspect of their proposal and for choosing a slightly different fork in the road than the one taken by the Progressive and New Deal traditions from which (among others) they draw.

First, in order to broaden and clarify the registers in which economic reasoning can inform law and policy, we should be clear that aiming to recover the tradition of classical "political economy" is not enough. Classical political economy—the tradition of Adam Smith and John Stuart Mill, among others—is understandably appealing to many present-day legal thinkers because it encompassed the study of the institutional and legal constitution of markets and economic life, and for that reason was interpermeable with the study of law itself. But it also ultimately pioneered the strange brainworm that has infected our thinking about the economy ever since: the notion that competition or competitive forces can determine market prices and other key economic outcomes on their own. As I have argued elsewhere, the origins of the antitrust tradition itself, both in terms of common law antecedents and antimonopoly politics, are better understood in terms of the more diffuse and democratically accessible traditions of "moral economy"—in which economic coordination is assumed, and competition is never presumed to be self-governing—than in terms of the elite tradition of political economy.

When the institutionalist economist Walton Hamilton cataloged the relationship between schools of economic thought for the *American Economic Review* in 1919, he identified both the new neoclassical economics and institutionalist economics—the latter being the ally and consort of progressive legal thought—as heirs to the classical economics of the previous century. Indeed, neoclassical price theory can be understood as a refinement and formalization of the concept of the self-regulating market in classical economics, while institutionalism can be understood as a continuation of the classical focus upon elucidating the legal and social structure of markets. The institutionalists (and the progressives more broadly) had an ambivalent relationship to neoclassical theory—sometimes repurposing it, often criticizing it, sometimes (as Alexander Hamilton did) suggesting that each could exist in its own lane. As we now know, that did not end up being a stable settlement: neoclassical economics displaced institutionalism in the United States entirely, only to later resurrect a hollow version of it in the "new institutionalism" (associated with the study of "transaction costs" that played a key role in the Chicago School antitrust revolution) that prized a particular conception of efficiency above all other considerations.

We have many good reasons, intellectual and pragmatic, to make a clean break from the neoclassical framework. We know—thanks to work in heterodox economics and the empirical study of firms and markets more broadly, informed by close attention to the role of law—that competition alone does not govern market behavior. Coordination both within and often beyond business firms settles on parameters, prices (or price ranges), and more. These market settlements periodically change or are disrupted, but we cannot have an honest study of the economy and markets—and of the law that deals with those things—without grappling with their existence. Keeping these matters firmly in view is central to achieving one of Fishkin and Forbath's goals: recapturing the democratic determination of economic life from narrow technocratic spheres.

Indeed, the contemporary legal and judicial consensus about the "constitutional" status of the Sherman Act and other antitrust statutes is *not* mainly built on the understanding that antitrust makes good on affirmative constitutional governance obligations to protect against oligarchy. It has rather become associated with deference to the very technocracy that the authors criticize. In other words, neoclassical law and economics itself has attained a kind of constitutional status, aided by judicial empowerment to make antitrust rules from the ground up. Fishkin and Forbath's constitutional arguments are a rich resource for deepening the arguments of advocates who are pushing back on both judicial and neoclassical economic supremacy in antitrust, in favor of an expanded role for the administrative state in implementing antitrust's broader egalitarian and democratic goals.

My second suggestion for extending the authors' arguments is closely related to the first. Progressives' ambivalence about emerging neoclassical theory was arguably intertwined with their optimism about the business firm as an engine of social and economic progress. With a few exceptions, they effectively assented to a kind of emerging legal hierarchy of economic coordination—led by the courts but mirrored in many reform efforts—with business firms as the gold standard. I call this the *firm exemption* because it entails an unwritten "exemption" not only from antitrust law—even as the terms of the "labor exemption" and other exemptions for more democratically constituted forms of economic coordination were being debated—but also from the competitive order of the neoclassical vision. Contemporary economic reasoning takes the firm as the basic unit of analysis, for many purposes treating it as a black box, on grounds of its alleged productive and technical efficiencies. But even if it were analytically coherent to trade off such efficiencies with the distinct concept of "allocative efficiency" that is deployed to undermine many other forms of economic coordination, regnant policy and legal frameworks do not consistently or fully entertain other forms of coordination that could also realize such efficiencies. As a result, these frameworks often cut off the ability of other forms of association to realize productive efficiencies.

When Robert Bork promoted a permissive posture toward mergers, he built upon an existing element in the structure of antitrust law as he found it. He pointed out, rightly, that firms were already preferred over equivalently sized cartels on the basis of their putative productive efficiency. From this vantage, the Chicago School selectively expanded the firm exemption through merger policy and the liberalization of vertical restraints. (The gig economy and other variants of the fissured workplace we know today are the direct results.) But the Chicago School didn't invent the firm exemption. It was developed much earlier, with progressives' assent.

To be sure, progressives wanted the firm to serve public ends and to become a locus of regulation. But they did not foresee that the baggage that came with the efficiency claims they had too credulously embraced would end up undermining their own regulatory aspirations. Too many progressives (Louis Brandeis was a notable exception) accepted highly generalized claims about "economies of scale" that, if they obtained at all, frequently did so not because of true technical efficiencies—more output for the same capital and labor put in—but because of behemoth firms' greater leverage and power to squeeze more out of workers and out of smaller firms in their adjacent markets. These arguments, often framed in broad deductive terms, ultimately implicated not just firm size but also questions of how firms are internally organized by the law. As a result, these "economies of scale" arguments ultimately served to help fuel the hollowing out of not only antimonopolist aspirations but many other progressive regulatory aspirations as well.

Paul

The antimonopolists were never interested just in small firms, but more generally in forms of economic coordination that fostered genuine solidarity rather than control and dominance. Contemporary antimonopoly thinker Zephyr Teachout, whom Fishkin and Forbath cite, has said that antimonopoly is fundamentally about recognizing that it's more effective to prevent concentrations of power in the first place rather than regulate them after the fact. A natural corollary of that insight—once we internalize the ubiquity of market coordination—is to frame democratic, egalitarian structures of economic coordination as goods in themselves, rather than as existing only to countervail existing concentrations of power (the best they will ever be without a clean break from current modes of law and economics thinking). Fishkin and Forbath help make legible a constitutional obligation to do so.

THE HARD QUESTIONS
Kate Andrias

JOSEPH FISHKIN AND WILLIAM E. FORBATH are right that we should in-
voke the Constitution to build a more democratic and egalitarian political
economy—not only because the Constitution is a powerful rhetorical tool
in political debates, but also because, notwithstanding its antidemocratic
features, the Constitution both enables and requires a more democratic,
equal, and inclusive society than the one we now have. Fishkin and Forbath are also right to argue that the left should not cede the Constitution's
meaning to the Court and that legislators and social movements should
challenge the Court's anti-egalitarian and antidemocratic jurisprudence.
By reminding Americans of a lost tradition, Fishkin and Forbath make
an important and timely contribution, unsettling assumptions that the
Constitution has always had a fixed, pro-business cast and that it is exclusively the province of courts.

Yet Fishkin and Forbath also largely leave for others the difficult
questions about what it would mean for progressives and liberals
to take up their call today. What exactly should a constitutional

argument for democracy of opportunity, or for particular reforms, look like? What's the relationship between the high-level claim that the Constitution requires a more equal and democratic society and constitutional text, history, structure, precedent, and other accepted (or rejected) modes of constitutional argumentation? How should members of Congress or the executive proceed when their views on constitutional political economy diverge from that of the Supreme Court? Should the power of the Court be cabined by institutional reforms such as those examined by the Biden administration's Supreme Court Commission? Should federal judges approach constitutional questions about political economy differently from members of Congress? What role do state legislators or state courts play? And how about the efforts of social movements to advance a more democratic understanding of the Constitution—what are the pitfalls and obstacles they face? These questions are beyond the scope of Fishkin and Forbath's argument here, but tackling them is essential to making progress on their important charge.

Take workers' rights, for example. One of Fishkin and Forbath's central prescriptions in their book, *The Anti-Oligarchy Constitution*, is to "build and maintain robust secondary associations like unions" in order to "challenge the political and economic dominance of the few" and to "open new channels of democratic politics that can circumvent the political power of the oligarchs and their allies"—aims they identify as part of the anti-oligarchy strand of the democracy-of-opportunity tradition. In their essay here, they also emphasize defending unions as a key component of "repairing the First Amendment." It's worth underscoring that unions are just as critical to other strands in the democracy-of-opportunity tradition, including racial and gender inclusion and building a robust middle class, not just the anti-oligarchy focus. Unions have the capacity to bring workers together across racial, ethnic, and gender divides in service of shared class interests, and they are critical to improving material conditions for all workers, particularly less powerful workers, while also advancing economic and political inequality more generally.

Fishkin and Forbath deftly build on the historical work of other scholars like James Pope and Laura Weinrib to show that past workers' movements and their allies invoked the Constitution to support the right to organize and strike, and they gesture to what revitalizing these arguments might look like today. But their argument operates at a general level, urging that justices and others embrace an "understanding of the constitutional necessity of countervailing power" when considering the First Amendment and labor. This is right, but only a start; the arguments for robust constitutional protection for labor rights—for what the dissent should have said in *Janus* and for a constitutional right to organize, strike, and picket—are actually much stronger, and more consistent with traditional modes of constitutional interpretation and even prior Court precedent, than they suggest.

As Justice Frank Murphy wrote in the 1940 case *Thornhill v. Alabama* when striking down a state law that criminalized labor picketing, labor speech deserves particular protection under the First Amendment: "labor relations are not matters of mere local or private concern. Free discussion concerning the conditions in industry and the causes of labor disputes appears to us indispensable to the effective and intelligent use of the processes of popular government to shape the destiny of modern industrial society." Or as Justice Felix Frankfurter argued in dissent in an early case involving a constitutional challenge to union dues, "To say that labor unions as such have nothing of value to contribute to . . . [the electoral process] and no vital or legitimate interest in it is to ignore the obvious facts of political and economic life, and of their increasing inter-relationship in modern society." In short, justices and other constitutional interpreters have in the past, and should again, embrace a more egalitarian understanding of the First Amendment, in the area of labor and beyond—one that recognizes the economic, political, and social inequalities that inhibit or enhance expression.

Moreover, a constitutional vision for labor rights going forward requires close attention to the efforts of contemporary on-the-ground worker movements. Such examination reveals that many worker movements are, in fact, challenging existing law and attempting to redefine labor activity like strikes as fundamental rights. And they are doing so in novel ways that can help shape future constitutional argumentation. Consider the remarkable union victory of Amazon workers in Staten Island in early April. In taking on the behemoth company, the workers, through their own newly formed union, challenged Amazon's right to authoritarian control at work and offered a vision for rights of speech and democracy in the workplace.

Also important is close analysis of the obstacles to building a progressive constitutional political economy. Fishkin and Forbath predict that, in the future, "conservatives will attack any new legislative protections for workers with novel legal arguments." In fact, that is already happening. The Supreme Court's recent trifecta of anti-worker cases (*Janus, Epic Systems,* and *Cedar Point*) is only part of the problem. In courts across the country, business groups are challenging democratically enacted statutes not only under the First Amendment, but also with novel uses of the Takings Clause, the Dormant Commerce Clause, the Supremacy Clause, due process, equal protection, and non-delegation, all in an effort to stymie state and local efforts to protect workers' rights.

Meanwhile, deep ideological divides pervade even the Democratic Party when it comes to labor. After all, in the period after the 1960s, Democrats didn't only abandon constitutional arguments about political economy, as Fishkin and Forbath lament; many also abandoned the working class altogether. As employers took advantage of weak labor law and worked to deunionize their workforces by permanently replacing workers who went on strike, moving production to nonunion areas and subcontracting to nonunion firms, and refusing to recognize new groups of workers who sought to organize, Democratic majorities in Congress offered little opposition. Today, despite significantly more support for labor within the Democratic Party and despite efforts at regulatory innovation by agency officials, key Democrats and many liberal elites continue to be tepid in their support for workers and for labor law reform. Few observers think the Protecting the Right to Organize Act (PRO Act) is likely to become law, at least in the near term.

The paucity of constitutional argumentation by Democrats about labor must be understood in this context. When legislators do not meaningfully support workers' efforts to unionize, strike, and win fair employment rights, it is wholly unsurprising that they don't make constitutional arguments about those rights. They haven't just forgotten to do so.

In short, Fishkin and Forbath are right to call for a new progressive constitutional political economy generally and for labor rights in particular. But as they recognize, changing the reality on the ground, whether regarding labor rights or other progressive ends, will require struggle and organizing; employing constitutional rhetoric is only one small part of the picture. It will also require tackling the hard questions about what a progressive constitutional vision actually entails.

FINAL RESPONSE
Joseph Fishkin & William E. Forbath

WE APPRECIATE all of these responses, for many different reasons, but one of them is simply that together the responses exemplify our highest aspiration for this book: that it will inspire others to do related work fashioning a version of the democracy-of-opportunity tradition for our own time.

It is going to take a lot of work. And that work will be, as Andrea Scoseria Katz describes it, decidedly "uphill." She is right that we aim to convince progressives to appreciate the "ineliminably political" nature of constitutional argument—and to disabuse themselves of the notion that the Supreme Court ought somehow be made to sit above politics, rendering judgments that ought to be defended from politics. Convincing progressives to reorient their view of politics and the Court in this way is not easy or quick. It is something like turning an enormous ship. But the Supreme Court may well help us out. The more damage the Court does to the country—the more nakedly it translates not just its reactionary vision of political economy, but really the whole agenda of one minoritarian political party, into constitutional doctrine—the more that vessel will turn. In other words, the Court's increasingly aggressive efforts to revive the Lochnerian constitutional political economy of the 1930s may ultimately help revive the constitutional politics of the 1930s, as well. We see our book, *The Anti-Oligarchy Constitution*, in part as a sourcebook, a set of resources for progressives to draw on, as this great shift creates more room and more need for progressive constitutional arguments in politics, outside of courts.

Part of the work will be, as Kate Andrias suggests, translating the claims about constitutional political economy that make up the democracy-of-opportunity tradition into the kinds of idioms of constitutional argument that contemporary Americans recognize. We think this work is easier in the field of labor that Andrias highlights than in most others. Structural claims about constitutional political economy were central to the tradition we describe (both in our essay here and in the book) but are a tougher fit for our present legalistic and court-centered constitutional world. Labor, however, has always made sharp and ringing claims about rights, many of them with deep roots in constitutional text. The right to organize, the right to strike, and the right to associate and to speak to one another have long been central to labor's constitutional case.

Americans understand these claims today, whether they agree or disagree with them—and whether or not courts are willing to vindicate them. We think the work these claims did on the ground in labor struggles, legislative arenas, and even in court is essential source material for those who wish to revive labor's constitutional claims today. Our book, in addition to exploring this source material, begins to sketch some of that work of revival. But as Andrias suggests, much more work is required. And quite a lot of it will be by labor activists themselves, along with political leaders.

Sanjukta Paul suggests that perhaps the idea of "political economy" is itself a bit too redolent of neoclassical notions for our purposes. She urges us to reach back, as she has done in other work, to the older idea of a "moral economy"—a term the great English historian E. P. Thompson coined to capture the notion that market relations are (or ought to be) embedded in and constrained by customary norms and conceptions of fairness. As a matter of terminology, we think "political economy"—and therefore "constitutional political economy"—is capacious enough to capture a wide range of positions and work, including Paul's. We do not write here on a blank slate. Instead, we write at a moment of extraordinary progress for a movement in law, political science, and related fields that sails under the "political economy" flag. For example, the Law and Political Economy (LPE) Project, to which several of the participants in this forum, including Paul, have contributed great work, has shown the power of political economy as a framework around which to build a movement. The core idea—that politics and markets are inextricably intertwined—is open-ended, and good for getting a variety of claims off the ground. We agree with Paul that as this field matures, the question of who is entitled to coordinate with whom—as among workers, employers, firms of various sizes and market positions, and so on—will be a central battleground of fights about constitutional political economy, and we appreciate her work developing the tools for analyzing this rich set of problems.

To be relevant today, the democracy-of-opportunity tradition will need to evolve and change quite a lot. This has happened many times before. This means inventing new policies and institutions to instantiate the democracy-of-opportunity tradition in a changing world; it also means reckoning with the tradition's tangled, tragic past, and the lasting effects of that past on the present. We agree with Aziz Rana: a rekindled democracy-of-opportunity tradition must once again widen its moral horizons and imagined membership. And this requires addressing the historical connections between several past eras of egalitarian political-economic reform and the concurrent political economies of slavery and of imperial conquest and neoimperial expansion. As we explore in the central chapters of the book, the Jacksonian democrats' early incarnation of the democracy-of-opportunity tradition tied its commitments to material freedom and independence for white male producers to the promotion of Black slavery and Indian removal. Reconstruction Republicans set out to change this tragic course of constitutional development, with new measures for and commitments to Black political and economic enfranchisement, but western expansion and conquest played a critical part in undermining them. And racial and gender subordination were wrought into, and in turn propped up, various aspects of the New Deal. (Historian Gabriel Winant's recent book *The Next Shift: The Fall of Industry and the Rise of Health Care in Rust Belt America* has highlighted the lasting marks of this New Deal history—and how much of today's political economy needs to be remade to undo them.)

But our book does not explore Rana's most provocative suggestion, that the mid-twentieth century moment of relatively broadly shared prosperity—at least among white men—was linked with U.S.

imperial projects abroad. Rana carefully notes that such connections were contingent facts of history, not "philosophical requirements." We agree. But the fundamental question he raises is whether it is possible in the future to build a democracy of opportunity that is not linked with a national policy of "belligerence" and "external power projection." We think the answer is yes. In part that is because there have always been powerful examples of efforts, as Rana puts it, to "wed anti-imperialism and democracy of opportunity," such as those of W. E. B. Du Bois and Martin Luther King, Jr.; these voices have been dissenting ones, but today we must bring them into the mainstream. The prospect for building a multiracial party of radical democratic reform, as uphill as this may be, is a great deal better now than it was during any past U.S. crisis of economic inequality. And only a radically more democratic and inclusive constitutional political economy on the domestic front can undergird the political conditions for a United States committed to creating the frameworks for a more democratic and egalitarian international political economy. Rana's forthcoming work on just this mighty problem will be an essential starting point for the reimagining it entails.

Finally, we certainly have not given, as Mark Tushnet puts it, a complete "progressive constitutional manifesto for the twenty-first century." We do not discuss a wide range of issues that any such manifesto definitely would cover, including some of truly existential urgency, such as Tushnet's first example of climate change. To be sure, a federal government that was reconstructed in some of the ways we advocate, with more power for Congress and less for the Supreme Court, would be dramatically more able to meet the challenge of climate change, because it would be more capable of acting in many spheres. But that is not the same thing as saying that addressing climate change is something the Constitution requires (beyond the obligation to secure the general welfare, of which this issue is surely an urgent part). We are more than open to some of the democratic innovations Tushnet offers, including using new mechanisms such as deliberative polls for democratizing and decentralizing the way policy is made. This kind of innovative institutional rethinking echoes and builds on some of the rethinking advocates working in the democracy-of-opportunity tradition did a century ago, during the last Gilded Age. But any such innovations will only be achieved through politics. And specifically, we would submit, through a politics that emphasizes the democratic strains in our Constitution.

We close this brief reply where we began it: with enormous gratitude to the respondents and renewed energy for the work that lies ahead.

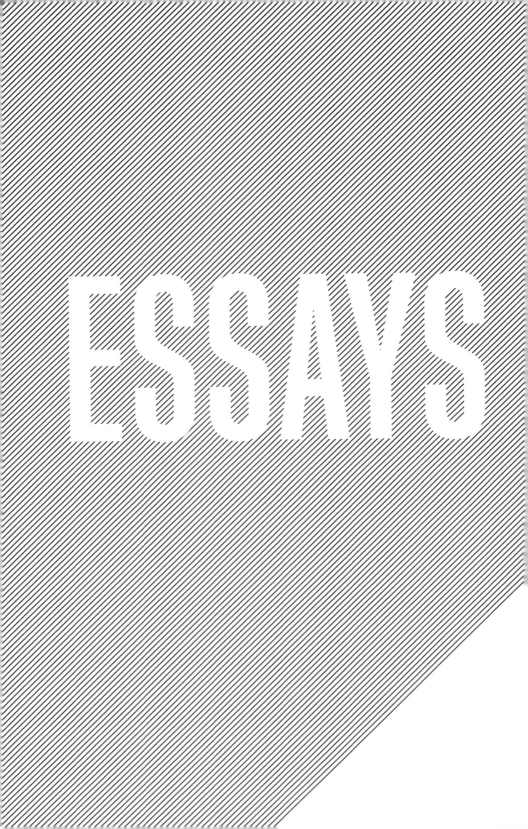

ESSAYS

WHAT MOVEMENTS DO TO LAW

Amna A. Akbar, Sameer Ashar,
& Jocelyn Simonson

IT HAS NEVER BEEN CLEARER that ideas germinated by social movements exert great force in law and politics in the United States. Examples from the left abound over the last decade. Occupy Wall Street mobilized people against growing economic inequality and laid a foundation for anticapitalist critique and socialist politics. Indigenous resistance from Hawaii to the Dakotas connected environmental justice to the revival of anticolonial politics. The Ferguson and Baltimore rebellions, combined with organizing by the Movement for Black Lives and a growing constellation of abolitionist organizations, have made anti-Blackness, white supremacy, and police violence core issues on the liberal-to-left spectrum and redefined the terms of policy debate. About five years ago, through direct action, disabled activists forestalled the repeal of the Affordable Care Act. As we write, Immigrations and Customs Enforcement announced the closure of Etowah County Detention Center in Alabama—a long-time site of abolitionist resistance. And through strikes and organizing, nurses, teachers, taxi and app-dispatched drivers, Amazon ware-house workers, and Starbucks baristas are reasserting worker power throughout the country.

Of course, this organizing on the left is matched—dwarfed even, in certain respects—by organizing on the right. Whether you call it frontlash, backlash, or retrenchment, the right is building on decades of organized infrastructures and consolidating considerable state power at the local, state, and federal levels. There are the attacks on the teaching of histories of enslavement and colonialism (mislabeled "critical race theory"), bans on speaking about trans and queer identities ("Don't Say Gay" laws), and the culmination of a long campaign to outlaw abortion. There is the racist expansion of Stand Your Ground laws and criminalization of left protest in a number of states. These efforts mobilize the right's base. All the while, the Democratic Party faithfully affirms notions of law and order, decrying those who call to defund the police as naïve and out of touch.

What role does the law play in this climate? From the housing and debt crises to the sprawling grip of the carceral state on all corners of life, it is plain that neoliberal law and politics have failed the majority of people in the United States. Unsurprisingly, court-centered strategies for progressive social change championed by liberal elites have proven ineffective at reversing neoliberal governance. The consolidation of a conservative supermajority on the Supreme Court forced some liberals to confront the limits of their belief in the courts. Alongside modest proposals for judicial reform, there are more critical arguments. Some who believe in emancipatory horizons argue that we must reduce the role of the judiciary within our politics and that the

Supreme Court is a fundamentally antidemocratic force; the answer is not to reinstantiate the courts' power in liberal guise but to reduce or abolish it altogether. This critique of courts is not limited to the Supreme Court. Across the country, social movement organizations are seeding campaigns to shrink the footprint of criminal courts, to challenge housing courts as eviction mills, and to obstruct family courts separating children from their families.

We think these are small steps in the right direction. The greatest hope of achieving the large-scale legal change needed to build a robust democracy lies in today's left social movements—their imaginations, tactics, and strategies for political, economic, and social change. Organizing and collective disruption are often thought of as being in opposition to the law and the order it imposes. There is indeed a tension there, but it is only through organizing from below that we might transform the antidemocratic structures that constrain emancipatory change.

In a recent law review article, we made the case to other legal scholars that we should think about law in and with movements—a distinctive form of legal thinking we call *movement law*. In our conception, movement law is not the academic study of social movements; it is a praxis that requires thinking and experimenting alongside movements.

Our formal institutions of law and politics are designed to serve Amazon's executives and shareholders, rather than the 1.5 million people who work for it; the cop and the prosecutor, rather than those they arrest and imprison; the pharmaceutical company, rather than the many people in need of lifesaving drugs. The question for those focused on law is how we relate to these formal institutions, what credence we give them, and how we build avenues of resistance and alternative institutional configurations. Law is not an apolitical body of rules to be parsed and applied by technical experts. The law is political and relational. Law is governed—in both design and enforcement—by unequal distributions of wealth and power. But it is productively shaped, too, by grassroots contestation, as recent books by Scott Cummings and Deva Woodly suggest.

Movement law draws on the experience of lawyering with and for movement formations. It also builds on jurisprudential schools of thought, including critical legal studies, critical race theory, and feminist legal theory. By looking to lived experience and structures of inequality, scholars such as Mari Matsuda and Kimberlé Crenshaw have long complicated conventional accounts of law—what it does and for whom and how it can and should change—with an eye toward collective struggle. Gerald Torres and Lani Guinier wrote about how social movement contestation can generate legal meaning. "Demosprudence," as they call it, describes how "mobilized constituencies, often at the local level, challenge basic constitutive understandings of justice in our democracy." Building on this work, movement law asks us to think alongside social movements as they struggle for power and produce emancipatory horizons.

Undoubtedly, this is a daunting moment in which to direct attention to movements. The left is in relative demobilization and disarray, despite some recent wins, including recent labor wins. But too much hangs in the balance to look away.

A FUNDAMENTAL AIM of movement law is to understand social movements' strategies, tactics, and experiments as pathways for justice. To understand that emancipatory horizons must be generated collectively and in relation to grassroots struggle.

Contemporary workers' movements, for example, are reconceiving relationships between workers, employers, and the state by pushing at the narrow parameters of collective action in the workplace as defined by the National Labor Relations Act (NLRA) of 1935. The NLRA was itself born of massive, disruptive, and sustained labor activism in the industrial workplaces of the early twentieth century. But courts interpreted the statute to constrain worker organizing in favor of capital. And Congress, partly in reaction to widespread strike activity following World War II, amended the NLRA in 1947, imposing rules of workplace organizing that further deterred collective action.

Working within this legal regime, contemporary workers' movements fight rearguard campaigns to preserve the eligibility of low-wage workers for current workplace protections while envisioning new ways to assert collective worker voice. In the last two decades, movement organizations have supported worker mobilization and collaborated with unions to secure contingent gains. Garment workers in Los Angeles have fought to establish joint liability for wage violations between well-known fashion brands and small manufacturers in their supply chains. Taxi workers in New York have engaged in multiple rounds of direct action to raise fares, forgive debt, and protest the Trump

"Muslim Ban." Domestic workers have struggled against isolation and multiple forms of subordination to pass bills of rights that raise labor standards in New York, California, and eight other states. Restaurant workers have taken on high-end chains and agitated against the $2.13 minimum wage for tipped employees. Tomato pickers in Florida have forced large fast food companies to raise wages and investigate sexual harassment in their supply chains. Amazon workers in New York and Alabama are currently trying to unionize their warehouses.

These efforts are significant, both in themselves and in relation to the law. Activist workers frontally attack technologies of workplace domination, reject a sharp divide between employment and labor law, and nurture grassroots worker leadership in social bargaining for more just workplace arrangements. They act both within and outside of the NLRA, adjusting to changing dynamics between employers and the state. They demonstrate that workers can overcome the constraints imposed by legal regimes on organizing *by* organizing. Thinking in conversation with such campaigns makes clear how grassroots contestation at the local level is central to the shape of law and legal entitlements. It illustrates the limits of established political and legal processes to represent working-class and poor people, and the power of capital in defining the terrain. And it demonstrates how movements enact change while building grassroots power.

Thinking with movements also allows us to see that even strategies around which the left has understandable hesitation may be retooled to build contingent power. The new right to counsel in eviction proceedings in New York City offers a case in point. It could be argued that this struggle, by focusing on assisting individuals in court rather than the broader structures that lead to eviction in the first place, will do more to legitimize the fundamentally unequal political economy that produces housing precarity than to render housing provision more just. This concern is sometimes known as "the critique of rights": the idea that the promise of individual rights cannot solve collective problems under a system of racial capitalism. The struggle for housing justice must be broader than the right to counsel, dependent as rights are on existing relationships of power and economy.

This does not mean, though, that struggles over the right to counsel cannot be a productive part of a larger fight. Indeed, as John Whitlow has recently written, a push for counsel can be part of a constellation of efforts to increase the power of organized tenants in the face of a larger crisis of housing and an incredibly powerful real estate industry. This is how, in New York City, tenants unions spanning from the South Bronx to Ridgewood, Queens, formed the Right to Counsel Coalition, developed a larger analysis of the housing court system, and aimed to disrupt the court process. All the while, constituent members of the coalition built their ranks and their organizational capacity. As a result, even though the Right to Counsel legislation has passed, the fight continues: through mutual aid and for good-cause eviction legislation; for meaningful state housing subsidies beyond one-time pandemic relief; and, more broadly, for a renewed claim for housing for its use value and as central to community safety.

Another insight that arises from attending to social movements is how they engage in experimentation with institutional and social forms, mutual aid networks, community bail funds, and worker organizing collectives. In this way, social movements not only attempt to organize a base but prefigure the economic, social, and political relationships of the world they are working to build. Because of the overwhelming power of capital and the disciplining force of the state, these experiments are often relatively small in scale or narrow in application. But they mark possible openings and ideas for strategies that can be scaled up.

Grassroots groups using collective action against the carceral state are important examples. These include cop- and court-watching groups that gather to document the everyday violence of state policing and criminalization; community bail funds that pool resources to bail out people who could not otherwise afford their freedom; and participatory defense collectives that support people criminalized by the state while building broader collective knowledge of criminal courts. Beyond criminal courtrooms, there are campaigns for people's budgets and community control of the police; there are grassroots efforts to create transformative justice responses to harm outside of policing and incarceration. Using strategies that destabilize the normative footing of the carceral state, organizers redefine concepts of harm, community, and public safety as they directly contest the racialized logic of criminal law enforcement. A "community bail fund," for example, repeatedly posts bail for strangers, demonstrating through collective action that what the state claims keeps the "community" safe—pretrial detention based on poverty—in fact creates communal harms. Such activism challenges the criminal law's central focus on individual behavior, creating space for social movements to build bonds of community solidarity and safety as they develop their political analysis and grow their power.

These projects of social transformation directly challenge prevailing legal and institutional arrangements and the structures and understandings that hold them in place. They create pathways for justice and fight for horizons otherwise made invisible in conventional accounts of law. And they point to the broad array of strategies and tactics central to justice projects focused on transformation.

One final lesson of movement law thinking is that movements remind us of alternative arcs of history, often ignored in legal and liberal discourse, of people collectively generating ideas and struggling to build alternative possibilities from the bottom up, often at great risk to their own safety. Embedded in these alternative arcs are rich intellectual traditions. How can thrive together on shared land and with multiple forms of life? How have people lived in these ways in the past? What past struggles over land, resources, and labor shape our current norms and laws? These questions are deeper than what traditional legal discourse and adjudicatory forums allow. And when juxtaposed with conventional legal structures, they allow for new, often revelatory, ways of thinking about law, the state, and justice.

Investigating histories of how past movements have engaged with the law can illuminate pathways for us today. Legal historian Aziz Rana, for example, tells the story of the Black Panther Party's 1970 constitutional convention as a way to denaturalize the constitutional veneration at the heart of U.S. political culture and to recover how people's movements have resisted the document. The convention is estimated to have been attended by at least 12,000 people, including members of the American Indian Movement, the Young Lords, and Students for a Democratic Society. For the Panthers, the convention was a rejection of the Constitution and its naturalization of Black people's "economic and political subordination." The Constitution attempted to sever Black people in the United States from anticolonial struggles around the world. Participants generated a new constitutional text, with demands that included reparations, the transfer of wealth, truth commissions, and expanded socioeconomic rights. The convention marked the United States as a colonial project and conjured the possibility of a radical alternative.

Contemporary social movement ideation generates similarly destabilizing critiques of our legal order, for example in the realms of policing and criminal law. The radical imagination of the Movement for Black Lives and a revitalized wave of abolitionist organizing have built on longstanding critiques of race and capitalism in the Black radical tradition. It is precisely because of the last decade of rebellious racial justice organizing that the framework of "racial capitalism"—developed by Cedric Robinson and anti-apartheid activists in South Africa before that—has found purchase both in the academy and beyond. Movement voices offer a distinct way of conceptualizing the radical imagination through which movements seek to de- and reconstruct law and the state.

AS THESE CASES suggest, movement law points to the contingency of the stories we tell about history, power, and our contemporary arrangements. It highlights the limitations of relying on traditional legal sources instead of attending to people's experiences, movement struggles, and narratives. And it reveals the inadequacies of liberal legalism and the violence of the law. It aims to disrupt the pathways of formal politics, and the faith in the courts to do right by the people. It identifies that social movements point the way toward new institutional arrangements and social relations.

A movement law orientation takes seriously the need to get the stories we tell right, and seeks to offer thick description of social movement activity and the normative frameworks that undergird such activity. By focusing on the lived experience of the people engaged in organizing, we recognize that we are accountable to them. When we identify and support ideas generated within progressive and left movements, we contribute to seeding policy discourse with radical aims. Movements can be coopted when they attempt to translate long-term organizing and mobilizing into policy programs; then, elected officials and bureaucracies appear to respond to mobilizations while altering as little as possible. NGOs, journals, foundations, and universities are skilled at using the material force of the current order to suppress and coopt disruptive efforts. Academic institutions increasingly rely on soft funding for centers and institutes that issue reports and advise state bodies. These initiatives rely on organized money—for example, the for-profit "gunshot detection" company Shotspotter funds multiple university research institutes—and tend to entrench the status quo. These initiatives often obscure the protest, rebellion, and organizing that made possible the shifts in ideation with which they engage.

In contrast, movement law helps protect the most far-reaching aspirations of radical collective thinking. Movement law has the capacity to resist compromise, prevent the dilution of programs of structural social change, and render policy shifts more politically durable. When we think, write, and act alongside movements, we help name and disrupt the everyday violence of law and shape the discourse in which we participate.

Social movements have marshaled some of the most profound changes in how we relate to one another and what we can expect of the state. They galvanize hope and collective action in a way that can guide people to face the material crises of our time. By taking our cues from social movements, the radical visions we develop—those whose scale matches the scale of the problems we face—can change what we think is possible both within and outside of the law.

HOW LAW MADE NEOLIBERALISM
Amy Kapczynski, David Singh Grewal,
& Jedediah Britton-Purdy

WE LIVE IN AN ERA of intersecting crises—some new, some old but newly visible. Since its arrival in the United States, the novel coronavirus has intersected with and magnified long-neglected problems: radical disparities in access to health care and the fulfillment of basic needs that disproportionately impact communities of color and working-class Americans, alongside a crisis of care for the young, elderly, and sick that stretches families and communities to the breaking point.

These crises arise from the chronic failure of political institutions to respond democratically to public needs. They are rooted in decades of politics, policy, and law. For many Black, brown, rural, Indigenous, and working-class Americans, this democratic failure is business as usual. But over the last four years, and especially since the storming of the Capitol, fear of democratic failure has become mainstream.

These crises are often analyzed in terms of the political economy of neoliberalism, an ideology of governance that came to predominate in the 1970s and '80s. Neoliberalism is associated with a demand for deregulation, austerity, and an attempt to assimilate government to something more like a market—but it never was as simple as a demand for "free markets." Rather, it was a demand to protect the market from democratic demands for redistribution.

This analysis of neoliberalism too often overlooks the critical role that law plays in constituting neoliberalism. Law is the essential connective tissue between political judgment and economic order.

Many people recognize that the law has changed in anti-egalitarian and antidemocratic ways in recent decades—for example, that *Citizens United* amplified the role of money in politics, or that the construct of "color-blindness" has become entrenched in constitutional doctrine and helps sustain structural racism. In our view these are not isolated changes, but part of an orientation—an ideology about markets, governments, and law that has become foundational to our legal infrastructure. We call this orientation the "twentieth-century synthesis" in legal thought.

Under the twentieth-century synthesis, areas of law that concern aspects of "the economy"—for example, contracts, corporations, and antitrust—were given over to a "law and economics" approach that emphasized wealth maximization. Meanwhile, other values—such as equality, dignity, and privacy—were supposed to be realized in constitutional law and areas of public administration. Shaped by these ideological currents, constitutional law turned away from concerns of economic power, structural inequality, and systemic problems of racial subordination. Other "public law" areas did the same. The result was that deep structures of power at the meeting place of state and economy were shielded from legal remedy and came to seem increasingly natural.

A number of us—legal scholars, practitioners, activists, and academics gathered under the rubric Law and Political Economy (LPE)—have begun rethinking the relationship between law, economy, and politics suggested by the twentieth-century synthesis. Our ambitious hope is to replace the current "common sense" of legal scholarship with a new set of default ideas that will prove more responsive to the crises that we face.

Law must move from trapping us in accelerating crises toward providing paths to new and more adequate ways of setting democratic terms for a common fate. The Constitution, for example, should be interpreted and amended to align with democratic principles and become a platform for actual democratic self-rule. Other changes—to constitutional doctrine, voting rights, and legislative procedure—are also urgently necessary if the country is to become more democratic. Simultaneously, lawyers must advance values of democratic empowerment in institutional settings that have, for decades, been defined as insular, technical, and, if at all political, relating to expert "governance." The twentieth-century synthesis has obscured the significance of this work. But, if we are to emerge from this era of crisis, we need legal thinking that operates on fundamentally different presumptions.

THE HISTORY OF postwar economics and its intellectual predominance are partly responsible for the growth of the synthesis. The synthesis is also a story of the relative economic success of the decades

Kapczynski, Grewal, & Britton-Purdy

following World War II, when the market economy seemed to be reliably expanding, with broadly shared increases in income. Both Democrats and Republicans increasingly came to see the economy as an object of routine expert management. Persistent issues of inequality, such as racial hierarchy, were recast by many mainstream thinkers in the 1950s and '60s as problems of inclusion in a system that basically worked. That idea persisted long after any empirical plausibility was undercut in the mid-1970s, when wages stopped increasing for ordinary workers. Its legitimacy was further undermined by the inequitable results of the financial crisis of 2007 and 2008, the aftermath of which persisted even as we careened into the COVID-19 recession.

The synthesis comprises three presumptions that structure much of conventional legal and policy discourse. The first presumption is that the economy is a potentially autonomous system in principle—self-correcting, efficient, and largely serving the common good. On this view, government "regulation" interrupts the system and should be treated with suspicion unless it simply solves "market failures." Those failures may be widespread, and the state's role in shaping and maintaining the economy extensive, but the law is to be oriented toward an approximation of the self-sufficient ideal of economic order. This presumption erases the growth of unequal income and wealth that is the empirical tendency of market economies, as well as the "private government" of managers dominating workers and monopoly firms, such as Amazon, increasingly dominating whole sectors of the economy. From this perspective, antitrust regulation gets between giants such as Amazon and their willing customers;

unions regiment the labor market, boxing out individual at-will employment; financial regulation curtails innovation among investment managers. This posits that liberty and the general welfare will be advanced by getting the state out of the way—by "deregulating."

Of course, the synthesis arose during an era not of deregulation but of selective reregulation. Certain parts of the state grew larger and more restrictive, redeployed to advantage the powerful few. For example, regimes of intellectual property and transnational investment protection—regulatory, if anything—were constructed to empower powerful businesses in the Global North. At the same time that the government scaled back social services, it deployed expensive systems of incarceration and penal welfare. The state refined systems of parole and child support to make poor people, disproportionately of color, "get to work or go to jail." Extractive immigration laws gave bosses more control and made workers, authorized and unauthorized, more vulnerable. The stories of Flint and Ferguson are not about deregulation and market freedom, but about privateering business interests finding a foothold in a degraded public sphere, implementing new ways to extract wealth from ordinary people, and denying basic entitlements to freedom, equal care, and democratic voice. The result has been the greatest economic inequality and concentrated economic power in a century. At every step, law has been central to these developments—not only providing the rules for new systems of extraction and upward redistribution, but also elaborating the ideas used to rationalize them.

The role of law in weakening the welfare state and expanding incarceration is clear, but the shifts in law and legal logic that operate further from the spotlight have largely been obscured. Take two examples from economic law: antitrust and labor law.

The Sherman Act, which regulates the level of concentrated ownership in any given industry, was passed and enforced on the theory that corporate concentration was a threat to democracy. Justice Louis Brandeis's perhaps apocryphal claim that "we may have democracy, or we may have wealth concentrated in the hands of a few, but we can't have both" could have served as a motto for the field. Beginning in the 1970s, under the influence of conservative scholars (including Robert Bork), antitrust law abandoned this original theory. In its place, it refocused on the goal of low prices (called "consumer welfare"). Antitrust law followed neoclassical economics in assuming that behemoths are generally large because they are delivering good value, not because they are accumulating too much power. This conviction also presumed that corporate shortcomings would be revealed by new competitors, reinterpreting the waning of competition as attributable to the efficiencies of dominant business. Now our banks are too big to fail, Amazon and Facebook are public infrastructures in private hands, and the meat industry engages in price gouging. This regime is not serving the general welfare, let alone the purposes of freedom and democracy that were once its anchors.

The keystone of twentieth-century labor law, the Wagner Act, was passed in 1935 to support the creation of unions and promote collective bargaining. As Senator Robert Wagner put it, "Democracy in industry means fair participation by those who work in the decisions vitally affecting their lives and livelihood." This idea of "industrial democracy" aimed to correct the "inequality of bargaining power" between workers and employers. For many decades it did just that, as unionization rates rose steadily in the decades following the act, peaking at about 35 percent in the 1950s and early '60s.

Today, with private-sector union membership at 6.3 percent, the most salient bodies of law for most employees have nothing to do with unions. Take for example the series of court decisions that allowed employers to extend arbitration agreements from disputes among companies and sophisticated actors to employer–employee disputes. This means that whatever rights employees theoretically have must be asserted in private forums that reliably favor employers. Another example is the permissive category of the "independent contractor," which both new companies (such as Uber and Lyft) and many longstanding outfits have used to reclassify those they employ as free agents—free, chiefly, from the legal protections employees enjoy.

A legal regime intended to balance power and promote democracy has given way to one that ignores the huge difference in power between companies and individual workers. Law ignores this discrepancy and, thus, deepens it. This shift in law has helped create our world of low-wage and insecure jobs that endanger workers' health and safety. As COVID-19 has shown, this endangers all of us.

The second presumption of the synthesis is that legal equality, especially constitutional equality, is best understood as formally equal individual treatment, against a backdrop of a market reified as natural, rather than in light of the deep, structurally conditioned, and market-embedded differences that actually constitute the lived experience of race, gender, and class hierarchies. Formal equality forbids explicitly differential treatment of individuals in different groups, such as Jim Crow segregation, which means that it effectively requires "everyone to play by the same rules" on an unequal playing field. Shaped by this premise, much of the modern jurisprudence of equality turns a blind eye to the cumulative weight of historical systems, biases, and policies that perpetuate disparities in wealth, health, power, and privilege—from the segregated structure of our cities to the racial wealth gap.

In the 1970s the federal courts asked whether the Constitution allowed unequal school funding, whether racial equality was consistent with "color-blind" policies that reproduced racial gaps, and whether Congress could undercut the effective right to abortion by banning abortion funding while covering the costs of childbirth with public funds. The Supreme Court answered "yes" to each question. Through these decisions, equality came to mean having the same opportunity to win or lose in the marketplace. But this was burdened, of course, by unequal histories of poverty and discrimination.

Finally, the third presumption of the synthesis was that democratic politics was best understood, in practice, as a vehicle of irrational and opportunistic decisions, which should be constantly subjected to technocratic and juristocratic oversight. Some of this skepticism reflects the influence of "public choice" theory, and some of it implicitly reflects a longer history of technocratic condescension to democratic publics. Skeptics believe that the public is too ill-informed and ill-equipped to handle modern complexities, contending that we instead need insulated expert decision-makers— whether at the Federal Reserve or the Supreme Court.

The public was redefined as a collection of discrete "interest groups," then shut out of rooms where trade deals were negotiated or interest rates were set. For example, reigning trade theory from the 1980s into the last decade asserted that all "interest groups" had to be held at bay—treating both citizens and corporations as "rent seekers" who would disturb the grand bargains and decrease efficiency. In practice, though, the public was shut out of treaty negotiations while corporations were brought to the inside and allowed to set the table. This resulted in trade regimes that gave capital priority—for example, access to transnational arbitration to protect their investments, to which labor had no similar claim.

But this logic was not limited to trade. Government during this period came to be seen not as a vehicle for public will, nor politics a place to debate, form opinions, and seek the public good. Rather, both were assimilated to the logic of the marketplace, where the only "rational" choice is maximizing one's own individual benefits. Here, government—with its monopoly on the use of force and certain public institutions—was a suspect kind of monopolist. Free from the disciplining force of "competition," it would inevitably become corrupt—a trough where "special interests" go to seek spoils.

On this thinking, it made sense to try to roll back government (read: labor and civil rights protections, environmental regulation, etc.) to enable market competition and have government function like a market. The Supreme Court and public institutions, enabled by both parties, blessed a range of moves to promote this ideal, most beyond the glare of constitutional law. This was the general rule: government would be rolled back at the same time that it was also rolled out. The point—sometimes implicit, sometimes explicit—was to enable market logics to rule over more of public life. All the while, the marketplace increasingly became a locus of concentrated power.

These three presumptions emerged from a combination of intellectual networks and, yes, interest group politics. On the one hand, scholarly debates about concepts such as cost–benefit analysis, economic efficiency, and public choice shaped the terrain of debates about law and public policy. Then, partisan actors and interest groups leveraged these debates to advance specific political agendas. Business lobbies used the rhetoric of efficiency, regulatory capture, and the veneer of academic expertise to lobby for policies that benefited their bottom line. The process was at many moments driven by the right and propelled by the power of well-funded formations—from the Olin Foundation to the Federalist Society. But these ideas could not have become hegemonic without key establishment figures on the left. It was President Bill Clinton, after all, who delivered workfare, "financial reform," and full-throated neoliberalism in international trade. It is only today that a position on money, budgets, and finance that could truly serve justice and democracy is starting to emerge from the wreckage of years when progressives conceded that there was no alternative to the neoliberal paradigm. The greatest success of neoliberal ideology may have been to make the state appear all the more like its caricature in neoliberal thought: the results provide more proof of the "failure" of the state and of democracy itself.

THERE ARE THREE PRINCIPLES that might help us move toward a new legal imaginary. Though these do not provide a methodology for scholarship or decision-making, they do represent a principled shift of legal inquiry to counter the precepts of neoliberal thought and the familiar discourses of legal neutrality. They also orient law toward a more democratic future, where the central task is not optimizing wealth and technocratic rule, but creating a more equitable and inclusive democracy and economy.

The first step is a reorientation from efficiency to power. Whereas, for decades, we have been asking what legal regimes are "efficient," we should instead be asking what regimes produce the kind of widely shared political and economic power that is fundamental to a democracy. This is not to insert politics and law where they were absent before, but rather to ask how we can deploy them toward the freedom of all, not just the ruling autonomy of a few. Markets are not "free"; they are riven throughout with power disparities which are, themselves, products of law and policy. We construct the kinds of markets we want—and that means that we should embrace the capacity of law and politics to construct a radically more inclusive politico-economic order.

This shift helps make sense of why, for example, a new approach to labor law and antitrust law should be central to a just political economy program. The revived attention being given to corporate power and anti-monopoly policy points toward a renewed use of public authority to check concentrations of private power. Similarly,

Kapczynski, Grewal, & Britton-Purdy

this commitment to rebalancing economic power manifests in the fights over worker rights—from their evisceration by measures such as Proposition 22 in California, to the efforts to expand labor's ability to organize and secure benefits for all. Labor law and the law of finance and money are suddenly among the most dynamic in the legal academy today, as LPE scholars have begun newly mapping the state power at the heart of our systems of market coordination, finance, and banking, and theorizing how they might be designed to distribute, rather than concentrate, power.

Second, we must recognize the ways that formal equality fails and ask how our laws might cultivate a deeper form of equity—the equality of status and dignity that comes from dismantling historical structures of class exploitation and racialized and gendered subordination. There are many challenges here. We must unravel how racism, the marginalization of social reproduction, and the coercion of care are entangled with our political economy. We must work against the grain of liberal thinking about inclusion that has deeply marked law and mainstream legal theory, and simultaneously against an older tradition of political economy that encoded a racialized and gendered conception of the nature of production and the economy. We must theorize the relationships between the carceral state and capitalism and ask how we can constitute democratic publics in a global system that was designed for exploitation and exclusion. We need to bring these insights to bear upon a constitutional tradition that enacts the very "encasement" of the economy to which we are opposed—all in the midst of a legal culture that celebrates tactics like litigation over strategies of movement-building and legislation.

But the generativity of this work is also clear, as scholarly debates about reparations, dismantling the carceral state, and intersectional strategies for labor organizing command a new conversation within and beyond the academy.

Third, we must limit the familiar anti-politics of legalism and technocratic decision-making through a commitment to democratic politics. Democracy has to mean more than the manufacture of public opinion alongside elections. At its heart it means that majorities set the country's direction, not the constitutionally gerrymandered pseudo-majorities of the Senate and Electoral College or the conclusions of neoliberal trade theory. Democracy also means deeper political empowerment, such as the capacity of communities to mobilize against the hoarding of political decision-making power in wealthier (and often whiter) constituencies.

How can we counter the power of technocratic elites without abandoning the need that any democracy has for expertise? And how can we build more participatory and inclusive political institutions without hampering the exercise of state power, and without simply reproducing class and racialized biases? As we reformulate the central question in fields such as administrative law, new campaigns for community benefits agreements, wage boards, and participatory budgeting are taking root. Emerging work emphasizes the relationship between social movements and law reform. At the same time that participatory politics and movement-building are critical to legal change, we must recognize that we cannot have a democracy without a commitment to constitutional forms. And democracy necessarily always means that our favored cause may lose.

Kapczynski, Grewal, & Britton-Purdy

Our three proposals for reorientation are not novel. They owe a great deal to prior generations of critical legal thought, critical race and feminist approaches to law, and prior waves of political economy scholarship dating back to legal realism and the Progressive Era. But in this moment of upheaval and crisis, it is crucial for legal thought and action to reclaim and foreground these orientations. They do not solve these problems; they draw attention to them and suggest terms in which we might engage them with our eyes on the right imperatives and hazards.

Indeed, recognizing the deep structural constraints that led to the present political crisis entails seeing that Donald Trump's presidency was less a catastrophic aberration than the culmination of long-standing ideologies—including, in law, the twentieth-century synthesis. If it were merely an aberration, we might hope that a good election cycle or two would get things "back on track" without fundamental change. But the counterevidence is all around us: President Joseph Biden's broadly popular Build Back Better plan, as well as voting rights and labor rights reforms, all ran abruptly aground in our counter-majoritarian Senate. A deeply conservative judiciary stands poised to entrench antidemocratic reforms still more firmly. Our enduring crisis, exacerbated by COVID-19, is clearly a symptom of unresolved structural inequities and forms of political disempowerment that stretch back centuries. And Trump's narrow 2020 defeat has only set the stage for more conflict in 2024 and the years to come, with no structural reforms that would enable popular will to have a more decisive role in the outcome.

The collapse of democratic politics into marketing and democratic rule into capitalist power; rampant inequality in a landscape of unmet needs; structural racism and other forms of subordination; the increasing weaponization of racism by political elites to help legitimize the hoarding of wealth; the still deferred creation of a community of equals capable of collective self-government: we must find ways to reckon with these failings and with the ideologies that have made them seem tolerable or even inevitable. Challenging the prevailing twentieth-century synthesis, and building legal theories and frameworks that can help bring about and sustain a more genuinely egalitarian democracy and economy, will have an essential role to play in this work.

The authors thank K. Sabeel Rahman for his collaboration on early drafts prior to his government appointment.

Kapczynski, Grewal, & Britton-Purdy

LEGISLATING REPRODUCTIVE JUSTICE
Rachel Rebouché

IN ONE OF ITS FIRST public statements, the Biden administration committed "to codifying *Roe v. Wade* and appointing judges that respect foundational precedents like *Roe*." This commitment anticipates a likely future in which the Supreme Court overturns constitutional protections for abortion rights—a reality that might materialize if the Court upholds a ban on abortion before viability. But any effort by the Biden administration to "codify" *Roe* in federal legislation will face deep political resistance and inevitably reflect some measure of compromise. And while President Joe Biden's pledge to protect *Roe* is welcome support of abortion rights, his terminology reflects a fundamentally misguided legislative aspiration.

Though the 1973 decision in *Roe* established a constitutionally protected right to abortion, it never guaranteed abortion access. The Supreme Court held only that state criminal laws banning abortion were an infringement of the constitutional right to privacy. Patients, in consultation with their physicians, could elect to have an abortion for any reason during the first trimester of pregnancy. In the second trimester states could regulate abortions in order to protect the pregnant person's health or the dignity of potential life, but after the second trimester, a state was permitted to ban abortion unless terminating the pregnancy was necessary to preserve the patient's life or health. This trimester system was abandoned in 1992, when the Court held that states could restrict abortion before viability—around twenty-four weeks of gestation—so long as the regulation did not place a "substantial obstacle in the path of a woman seeking an abortion of a nonviable fetus." The Court's decision to reject *Roe*'s trimester framework nevertheless claimed to preserve "the essential holding of *Roe*."

Given this history, current proposals to "codify" *Roe* could mean one of two things. On the one hand, it could mean establishing abortion as a statutory right to privacy, which is a basis of Supreme Court decisions that appeal to the Fourteenth Amendment. It could also mean creating a statutory framework for abortion rights tethered to fetal viability. Both approaches—even if politically successful—could make subsequent federal legislation out of touch and out of date. Instead of seeking to codify *Roe*, we ought to enact policies that strengthen the infrastructure for delivering abortion services.

FIRST, as many have long argued, a right to privacy is an inadequate anchor for abortion rights. Privacy undergirds an individual's freedom from government interference when choosing to end a pregnancy, yet it demands nothing from the state to support the realization of that choice or to create the conditions that ensure access to abortion. This insight has informed a shift in focus from reproductive rights to reproductive justice—the latter stressing that privacy rights are only valuable for people who can exercise them and emphasizing the needs of people oppressed, marginalized, and excluded by law.

Second, statutory rights based on a trimester or viability framework could, in practice, fail to thwart various state restrictions on abortions—restrictions that could proliferate if *Roe* is no longer the law of the land. For example, some state laws dictate that people must receive counseling or undergo superfluous medical procedures and tests before getting an abortion. Other laws single out abortion clinics and providers for financial and logistical burdens that are not typically imposed on other health care sectors.

By contrast, the Women's Health Protection Act (WHPA) illustrates how modern abortion legislation could go well beyond merely "codifying *Roe*." In a few of its provisions, the bill addresses specific restrictions on abortion, such as unnecessary waiting periods, inaccurate informed consent materials, pointless and expensive in-person visits, and restrictions placed on why people might have an abortion. If enacted, the bill would give providers the right to offer abortion care, and their patients the right to receive that care, free from state regulations that impede access and treat abortion differently than similar health care services. States passing new laws would have to show that regulation makes abortion services significantly safer or protects patients' health.

Unfortunately, though the bill was passed by the House last September, it failed to progress in the Senate earlier this year. Still, supporters remain hopeful that WHPA will gain traction if the Supreme Court overturns (or eviscerates) *Roe* and as reproductive justice becomes a significant issue for the November midterm elections. WHPA's sponsors must be aware, however, that any such proposal might not be able to withstand a challenge before the Supreme Court. Although WHPA drafters wrote a bill with prospective litigation in mind, one can easily imagine the arguments that anti-abortion states would make in challenging WHPA's legality.

Despite these political and legal obstacles, the struggle to enact federal legislation is in itself worthwhile. Proposed legislation such as WHPA is remarkable, regardless of its achievability, because of the commitments to reproductive justice that it articulates and draws together. WHPA represents a distinctly intersectional approach; it acknowledges that not all people who become pregnant identify as women. The bill embraces the idea that abortion care is a public health issue deeply connected with economic and racial justice. These acknowledgments are major steps forward. The bill does not merely aim to codify *Roe,* but also foregrounds the lessons learned since the decision by blocking current laws that prevent people from receiving care and anticipating future measures that will undermine abortion rights.

Yet for all these important features, it is notable that WHPA does not guarantee funding for abortion services. Many Americans in fact already live in a "post-*Roe*" country, either lacking meaningful access to abortion care or the ability to pay for the care they might be able to find. Such barriers create serious public health problems while simultaneously entrenching economic and racial inequality. Some 75 percent of people who terminate pregnancies survive at or near the federal poverty line, and a majority of those people report that the cost of raising a child is their chief reason for ending a pregnancy. This should not come as a surprise, given the financial insecurities that dictate the lives and choices of an ever-increasing number of people in the United States. Moreover, most abortion patients are people of color, who are overrepresented among the poor in this country due to centuries of racism.

When people cannot obtain abortion care, they incur social, financial, and physical costs that are extremely difficult to bear and have demonstrable long-term effects that perpetuate cycles of disadvantage and subordination. The COVID-19 pandemic has only amplified these burdens by rendering caregiving responsibilities even more challenging, worsening widespread unemployment and placing increased stress on an already overburdened health care system.

A bill introduced but that has not moved out of the House or Senate, the Equal Access to Abortion Coverage in Health Insurance (EACH) Act, aims to alleviate some of the costs of and barriers to abortion. The bill would require coverage for abortion care through public health insurance programs (such as Medicaid) and for federal employees. The bill also mandates that federally supported health care facilities provide care for eligible individuals and prohibits the federal government from inhibiting state, local, or private insurance plans from covering abortion services. The EACH Act addresses the longstanding prohibition of using federal dollars to pay for abortion care except for limited exceptions—a budget rider known as the Hyde Amendment. Although the Biden administration pledged to abandon the Hyde Amendment, the rider remains in force after a compromise to pass a 2022 budget.

The EACH Act would not only transcend yearly budgetary negotiations but also acknowledge the extent to which law influences health outcomes and reflect the reality that abortion restrictions entrench inequality. This kind of vital work may not be furthered by statutes tied to *Roe* or even by the Supreme Court's privacy jurisprudence. On the contrary, the highest goals of reproductive justice depend on the communities and networks of people who are rightly outraged by the assault on abortion rights. Federal action to protect abortion access across states and extend funding for services is important. But even were that legislation politically infeasible, statutes alone will not be enough to change the current political, economic, and social realities that obstruct abortion services.

ABORTION RIGHTS DEPEND as much upon the on-the-ground interventions that open avenues to care as they do federal rights. The threat to constitutional abortion rights and the difficulty of enacting legislation make that clear.

Increasing access, for example, need not depend on traditional means of obtaining abortion services. Abortion providers and advocates have mobilized quickly during the pandemic, alongside many other sectors of the health care industry, to provide care through telehealth. In July 2020 a federal district court lifted the Food & Drug Administration's (FDA) requirement that patients pick up the first drug of a medication abortion—the two-drug regimen that ends a pregnancy at or before ten weeks—at a health care facility during the pandemic. After the decision, remote care for abortion expanded and entirely virtual clinics began offering no-touch abortions. Growth of virtual care stalled after the Supreme Court stayed the district court's order pending the appeals process. But with new leadership at the FDA, persuaded by the evidence of tele-abortion's safety and efficacy, the agency suspended enforcement of the in-person rule for the course of the pandemic. Then, in December 2021, the FDA lifted the requirement that mifepristone, the first pill in a medication abortion, be picked up in person, clearing the way for supervised mail delivery and a new form of certified pharmacy dispensation.

As health care providers are increasingly able to administer care remotely, and pregnant people can self-administer abortions with minimal professional intervention, the map of abortion access has begun to change in ways that will outlast the pandemic and could withstand decisions by the Supreme Court. Such developments go far beyond anything *Roe* ever contemplated.

Given these potentially transformative opportunities, legislators would do well to provide funding and practical support that can ensure access to abortion care inside and outside of clinics. Extending telehealth for abortion, as well as self-managed care, would do much to address inequalities and increase access, two issues that have kept reproductive health care out of reach for many. It is time to stop talking about *Roe* as the touchstone for abortion rights and to start imagining what law and policy can do to facilitate affordable and available services.

WHAT MAKES LAWS UNJUST?
Randall Kennedy

AMONG THE COMMENTARIES that most dramatically frame the tension between law and justice are Martin Luther King, Jr.'s "Letter from Birmingham Jail" (1963) and subsequent critiques by jurists, most notably from future Supreme Court justice Lewis F. Powell, Jr.

King composed "Letter from Birmingham Jail" while imprisoned for leading a demonstration in defiance of an injunction in Birmingham, Alabama, on Good Friday 1963. He wrote it over the course of a week, scribbling on whatever scraps of paper he could scrounge before handing the notes to his lawyers for a secretary to type them out. Drafts would then be sent back to King for revision.

The letter responded to a statement by eight white clergymen published in January 1963. With school desegregation rulings looming, the eight men had urged white people to eschew protest in the street and instead take their complaints to court. Three months later, in the midst of King-led demonstrations, they wrote again, this time criticizing "a series of demonstrations by some of our Negro citizens, directed and led in part by outsiders. We recognize the natural impatience of people who feel that their hopes are slow in being realized. But we are convinced that these demonstrations are unwise and untimely." In their view, segregation in Birmingham could be best addressed by "citizens of our own metropolitan area, white and Negro, meeting with their knowledge and experience of the local situation." Again the clergy urged dissatisfied parties to bring their cause to the courts and to forgo protests. "We appeal to both our white and Negro citizenry," the eight proclaimed, "to observe the principles of law and order and common sense."

King's response was not wholly spontaneous. The year before, the *New York Albany News* had solicited a letter from him during his jailing in Albany, Georgia. Prior to that he had considered publicly rebuking southern white moderate religious leaders. In Birmingham, facing censure from white clergy, King finally delivered that rebuke. Featuring the logic and rhetorical moves of a well-written brief, the letter repeatedly disputes the accuracy of King's adversaries. He maintains that, even if their claims had been accurate, their arguments would still be deficient.

First, King denies their charge that he is an interloper, pointing out that his Southern Christian Leadership Conference (SCLC) had a Birmingham affiliate and that, indeed, the head of that affiliate, Reverend Fred Shuttlesworth, had invited King to town. More fundamentally, however, King challenges the insider–outsider dichotomy. "I am in Birmingham," King wrote, because "injustice is here" and "injustice anywhere is a threat to justice everywhere."

King similarly challenges the accuracy of the clergymen's contrast between his purportedly extreme conduct and the putatively restrained behavior of city officials, including the police. Elaborating on why the contrast "profoundly" troubles him, King responds:

> I doubt that you would have so warmly commended the police force if you had seen its dogs sinking their teeth into unarmed, nonviolent Negroes. I doubt that you would so quickly commend the policemen if you were to observe their ugly and inhumane treatment of Negroes here in the city jail; if you were to watch them push and curse old Negro women and young Negro girls; if you were to see them slap and kick old Negro men and young boys; if you were to observe them, as they did on two occasions, refuse to give us food because we wanted to sing our grace together. I cannot join you in your praise of the Birmingham police department.

King asserts as well that he, Reverend Shuttlesworth, and other activists had negotiated in good faith with public and private authorities in Birmingham only to see agreements betrayed.

More importantly, King challenges the premise that friction and unrest are necessarily bad, and that extremism is a vice. He insists that the social unrest that so perturbed the eight clergymen should have been seen as a hopeful sign—that long-oppressed Black people were challenging their subordinated status. "The present tension in the South," King contends, "is a necessary phase of the transition from an obnoxious negative peace, in which the Negro passively accepted his unjust plight, to a substantive and positive peace, in which all men will respect the dignity and worth of human personality."

As for the allegation that the SCLC's disruptive demonstrations constituted "extreme" measures, King boldly adopts the charge:

> Was not Jesus an extremist for love. . . . Was not Amos an extremist for justice. . . . So the question is not whether we will be extremists, but what kind of extremists we will be. . . . [T]he nation and the world are in dire need of creative extremists.

Having addressed critics' complaints, King sets forth some of his own, focusing on the white "moderate" as the obstacle to racial justice:

> I have almost reached the regrettable conclusion that the Negro's great stumbling block in his stride toward freedom is not the White Citizen's Counciler or the Ku Klux Klanner, but the white moderate, who is more devoted to 'order' than to justice[,] . . . who constantly says: 'I agree with you in the goal you seek, but I cannot agree with your methods of direct action'[,] . . . who constantly advises the Negro to wait for a 'more convenient season.'

Even more disappointing, King maintains, was the white ministerial moderate. Having hoped that southern white ministers, priests, and rabbis would be among his staunchest allies, King found that "some have been outright opponents" and that "all too many others have been more cautious than courageous," remaining "silent behind the anesthetizing security of stained glass windows."

Singling out a term—"law and order"—that would gain significance in the sixties and after, King writes that he "had hoped that the white moderate would understand that law and order exist for the purpose of establishing justice." When law fails to be just, King declares, it may be properly and nonviolently defied. "I

Kennedy

would agree with St. Augustine," he avers, "that 'an unjust law is no law at all.'"

A just law, he writes, "is a man made code that squares with the moral law or the law of God. An unjust law is a code that is out of harmony with the moral law. . . . Any law that uplifts human personality is just. Any law that degrades human personality is unjust." According to King: "All segregation statutes are unjust because segregation distorts the soul and damages the personality. It gives the segregator a false sense of superiority and the segregated a false sense of inferiority." Seeking to sharpen the distinction, King suggests two telltale indicia of legal immorality. One is that unjust laws typically entail "a code that a numerical or power majority group compels a minority group to obey but does not make binding on itself." A second is that unjust laws typically are "inflicted on a minority that, as a result of being denied the right to vote, had no part in enacting or devising the law."

Finally, King insists on distinguishing his disobedience of law from that of his antagonists: "In no sense do I advocate evading or defying the law, as would the rabid segregationist. That would lead to anarchy. One who breaks an unjust law must do so openly, lovingly, and with a willingness to accept the penalty."

King maintains that his precepts evinced reverence for acceptable law properly understood: a person "who breaks a law that conscience tells him is unjust, and who willingly accepts the penalty of imprisonment in order to arouse the conscience of the community over its injustice, is in reality expressing the highest respect for law."

FOUR YEARS AFTER King wrote "Letter from Birmingham Jail," the Supreme Court upheld King's conviction for contempt of court even if the injunction he violated was itself illegal. When Justice Potter Stewart quipped in the case, *Walker v. City of Birmingham*, that "respect for judicial process is a small price to pay for the civilizing hand of law," he sided with those who feared that protest had gotten out of hand; who believed that assertions of individual conscience had degenerated into egotistical pretensions; who held that talk of civil disobedience threatened to unleash chaos, and that attraction to King and sympathy for the sufferings of African Americans had tempted too many to abandon conventions that are crucial to stability in a large, complex, conflicted polity.

Scores of observers echoed these beliefs. One was Morris I. Leibman, a major figure in the Chicago bar, who in 1964, as chair of the American Bar Association Standing Committee on Education Against Communism, delivered an address pointedly titled "Civil Disobedience: A Threat to Our Law Society." Concerned about communist exploitation of racial conflict, Leibman insisted that "never in the history of mankind have so many lived so freely, so rightfully, so humanely." Our "imperfections," he declared, "do not justify tearing down the structures which have given us our progress." Challenging two rallying cries he associated with the Black freedom movement, Leibman excoriated "Freedom Now" and "righteous Civil Disobedience." The former, he charged, was a dangerous delusion: "The cry for immediacy is the cry for impossibility. It is a cry without memory

Kennedy

or perspective. Immediacy is impossible in a society of human beings. What is possible is to continue patiently to build the structures that permit the development of better justice." Leibman then declared that "the concept of righteous civil disobedience . . . is incompatible with . . . the American legal system." Our grievances, he insisted, "must be settled in the courts and not in the streets."

In "Civil Rights – Yes; Civil Disobedience – No (A Reply to Dr. Martin Luther King)" (1969), Louis Waldman, a liberal attorney, maintains that those who appeal to the legal system for relief against mistreatment "cannot say that they will abide by those laws which they think are just and refuse to abide by those laws which they think are unjust. And the same is true of decisions on constitutional principles." Contrary doctrine, Waldman declares, not only veers into illegality, but is also "immoral, destructive of the principles of democratic government, and a danger to the very civil rights Dr. King seeks to promote." According to Waldman, it was time for the organized bar to "tell Dr. King and his devotees of civil disobedience that the rule of law will and must prevail, that violators of the law, however lofty their aims . . . are not above the law."

Lewis F. Powell, Jr., president of the American Bar Association in 1964-65, offered consequential contribution to this camp of criticism. In a lecture delivered at the Washington and Lee University School of Law in April 1966 called "A Lawyer Looks at Civil Disobedience," Powell confronted what he termed the "heresy" of civil disobedience, the notion that "some laws are 'just' and others 'unjust;' that each person may determine for himself, in accordance with his own conscience, which laws are 'unjust;'

that each is free to violate the 'unjust' laws—provided he does do peacefully."

Powell expresses disappointment with what he perceives as the bar's complacency in the face of a dangerous provocation. "One would have supposed," he declares, "that lawyers . . . the guardians of our legal system, would have rallied promptly to denounce civil disobedience as fundamentally inconsistent with the rule of law." Instead, "most lawyers have remained silent," while "a surprising number have written in justification."

Powell—a southern moderate—writes that he appreciated "the deep emotions engendered by the civil rights movement."

> The negro has had, until recent years, little reason to respect the law. The entire legal process, from the police and sheriff to the citizens who serve on juries, has too often applied a double standard of justice. Even some of the courts at lower levels have failed to administer equal justice. Although by no means confined to the southern states, these conditions . . . have been a way of life in some parts of the South. Many lawyers, conforming to the mores of their communities, have generally tolerated all of this, often with little consciousness of their duty as officers of the courts. And when lawyers have been needed to represent defendants in civil rights cases, far too few have responded.

There were also the discriminatory state and local laws, the denial of voting rights, and the absence of economic and educational opportunity for the Negro. Finally, there was the small and depraved minority which resorted to physical violence and intimidation.

These conditions, Powell acknowledges, "have sullied our proud boast of equal justice under law." They "set the stage for the civil rights movement." They account, in large part, for why King's call for civil disobedience resonated so widely. Still, notwithstanding these extenuating circumstances, the heresy of civil disobedience, Powell warns, could in the end produce "even greater injustice" than the evil of white supremacism.

Powell's critique rests on three points. First, while flawed, U.S. democracy is sufficiently inclusive and regenerative to nullify calls for revolution. "Despite some conditions of injustice" in the United States, Powell contends, "wrongs can be and ultimately are redressed in the courts, the legislatures and through other established political institutions."

Second, Powell stresses that the appeal to transcendental values above "mere" law—the appeal to "natural law," "God's law," and "Justice"—was by no means accessible only to those whose ends one might find appealing. Segregationists, too, could make appeals to their version of God's law. Borrowing from a colleague, Powell writes that "if the decision to break the law really turns on individual conscience, it is hard to see in law how Dr. King is any better off than former Governor Ross Barnett of Mississippi, who also believed deeply in his cause and was willing to go to jail."

Third, Powell argues that civil disobedience ultimately undermined the Black freedom struggle. Though he concedes that civil disobedience might sometimes accelerate the pace of reform, he argues that its costs would generally outpace its benefits "in terms of racial bitterness and discord, and particularly in the . . . lawlessness . . . which the doctrine of disobedience has encouraged." Echoing

King's commitment to nonviolence, Powell insists that worthy ends "can never justify resort to unlawful means."

More than many of King's detractors, Powell acknowledges some of the gross injustices to which King alludes in his letter. One looks in vain, however, for a speech or article by Powell dedicated principally to repudiating white supremacism. His critique of evasion and defiance of the law by segregationists is sharp but ultimately parenthetical. It occupies a couple of paragraphs that are swallowed up by his main concern: rejecting King's justification for extralegal resistance to the racist status quo. As between the imperative to challenge racial oppression and perceived deficiencies of antiracist protest, the latter most firmly gripped Powell's attention.

Powell had had ample opportunity to condemn segregation and other manifestations of racial mistreatment. He was a lawyer-statesman with national prominence; served as chair of the Richmond School Board between 1952 and 1961 and president of the American Bar Association; he could be loudly insistent on many topics. In condemning white supremacism, however, Powell was diffident. While he noted for example, that southern legislatures and officials may have disobeyed the law first by refusing court-ordered school integration, this observation is merely a momentary digression. Powell's main point was that the United States, for all its flaws, is a democracy that morally warranted obedience from all its citizens, including Black people.

King did not dispute that point. He, too, pledged fealty to the United States; he displayed his devotedness by insisting upon accepting punishment for disobedience. Like Powell, King was a thoroughgoing patriot. Unlike King, however, Powell was not an impassioned enemy of racial oppression. He was, at most, a reserved adversary, condemning some of white supremacism's most obvious manifestations. But he did not seem to appreciate the breadth, depth, and destructiveness of racial oppression. One might not pick up from Powell's article, for example, that at the very moment of its publication, Virginia continued to punish marriage across the race line as a felony. What most stirred Powell was not the persistence of racism embodied in law, but perceived deficiencies in the thinking of racial dissidents. The lawyer's thinking reflected the sensibility that King directly chastises in his letter—the impulse of the white moderate "who is more devoted to 'order' than to justice," and "who constantly says: 'I agree with you in the goal you seek,'" but not the methods of direct action.

Powell charges King with offering little in his letter that distinguished "good" from "bad" law other than subjective preferences. Echoing Justice Hugo Black, Powell argues that it would be better for the country and Black America for racial justice activists to entrust their demands to democratically sanctioned legal procedures than ad hoc dramatizations on the streets. Further echoing Justice Black, Powell warns that the inclination to act as one pleases, notwithstanding law, would be considerably strengthened by applause for appeals to sources above legality.

"A Lawyer Looks at Civil Disobedience" reflects King's success, at least partially, in persuading Powell that the Jim Crow regime was morally rotten and that the rottenness reached deep into the ranks of the bar. Powell draws the line, however, at thought and conduct that repudiated key tenets of a legal regime that, to him, was flawed but essentially good. Powell never questions the ability of U.S. courts, laws, and political institutions to serve justice, and he argues that "due process and democratic procedures, even though painfully slow at times, are a far more dependable and certainly less dangerous means of correcting injustice and solving social problems" than acceding to ad hoc demands backed up by threats of civil disobedience.

Interestingly, despite Powell's rejection of King's argument for basing action in a "higher moral law," the protests that King's movement undertook did not, for the most part, defy federal law. Many observers associate the theory of civil disobedience that King advanced in the letter with the whole of direct action by the civil rights movement. Burke Marshall usefully noted, however, that racial dissidents defying Jim Crowism after 1954 most often were acting not against, but with, the law. They may have defied local segregationist ordinances, but they were typically doing so with the backing of a superior legal authority—the Constitution. There were many sit-in arrests, for example. But convictions were often annulled when appellate courts held that, under federal constitutional laws, local police had acted wrongly. The protest program, Marshall observes, typically "involved nothing that was illegal in an ultimate sense." True, participants expected that they would be arrested and jailed. But they expected this not because they intended to break any constitutional laws. They usually acted under a claim of federal constitutional right, and their legal prognosis was often proven correct.

Indeed, in his first major address as a civil rights leader, the extemporaneous sermon on December 5, 1955, in which he announced the Montgomery bus boycott, King appealed to the Constitution in understanding the difference between just and unjust actions.

> My friends, don't let anybody make us feel that we are to be compared in our actions with the Ku Klux Klan or with the White Citizens Council. There will be no crosses burned at any bus stops in Montgomery. There will be no white persons pulled out of their homes and taken out on some distant road and lynched for not cooperating.

He went on to say that "there will be nobody . . . among us who will stand up and defy the Constitution of this nation." What seems to have emboldened him to make such a claim was a perception of the Constitution as some sort of holy writ. "We are not wrong in what we are doing," King asserted. "If we are wrong, the Constitution of the United States is wrong. If we are wrong, God Almighty is wrong."

Eight years later, when writing "Letter from Birmingham Jail," King avoided resting his case on the Constitution as interpreted by the Supreme Court. Although he had typically deferred to what lawyers posited as the legal boundaries within which he could act, in Birmingham (as on several other occasions), he disregarded attorneys and was prepared to violate injunctions in accord with what he perceived to be "higher moral law." In jail, with the time and solitude needed to produce his defense of civil disobedience, King attended to the chore of distinguishing what makes a higher law, and why the character of his protest differs from that of white supremacists. He did not repeat his earlier suggestion that the Constitution was touched by divinity.

Rather, he rested his case squarely on the proposition that he was morally entitled to disregard immoral law, to act against a law that "conscience tells him" is unjust.

DESPITE KING'S EFFORTS, however, he could not accomplish what scores of philosophers and theologians have also failed to—creating a consensus metric by which to distinguish moral from immoral law in a large, diverse, and polarized society. King could not escape the reality that his distinction between just and unjust laws was ineluctably controversial. Powell was correct to note the danger that King's certitude posed: Governor Ross Barnett, a devout, church-going, Christian segregationist was also filled with certitude.

King, however, rightly recognized the universal need for an appeal to authority that transcends the established norms of government. As he observed, the atrocities that Hitler committed were "legal" under the laws of the Third Reich. King had the moral high ground, but he and Powell had latched on to different horns of an unresolved and unsolvable dilemma.

Kennedy

QUEER LIBERATION, IN AND OUT OF THE LAW

Mary Bernstein

DECADES OF LEGAL GAINS for LGBTQ people are on the brink of being reversed. Texas governor Greg Abbott recently issued an executive order declaring that gender-affirming care for minors constitutes child abuse and directed social service agencies to commence investigations. After several investigations had started, a Texas state court issued an injunction temporarily halting those inquiries, but the future remains uncertain. Arizona just passed a similar law banning gender-affirming care for children. Meanwhile, not to be outdone, Florida enacted what opponents call a "Don't Say Gay" bill banning the discussion of sexual orientation and gender identity in grades K–3. Taking a page from Texas's recent anti-abortion law, the law also affords parents greater opportunity to take legal action against school districts that they think violated the law.

That's just the start of it. The Supreme Court may overturn *Roe v. Wade* when it hands down its forthcoming decision in *Dobbs v. Jackson Women's Health Organization.* Ominously, Texas Right to Life advised in its *Dobbs* amicus brief that the Court should not "hesitate to write an opinion that leaves" decisions such as 2003's *Lawrence v. Texas* (which overturned bans on consensual sexual relations between same-sex adults in private, the so-called anti-sodomy statutes) and 2015's *Obergefell v. Hodges* (which legalized gay marriage) "hanging by a thread" because they "are as lawless as Roe." The days of *Lawrence* and *Obergefell*—and more recently *Bostock v. Clayton County*, which ruled against firing someone based on their sexual orientation or gender identity—may be numbered.

At first blush, the legal peril in which LGBTQ people find themselves might seem to confirm the worst fears expressed by progressive critics of legal strategies in movements for social justice. Rights can be granted, such critics emphasize, but rights can also be taken away. According to this line of thought, progressive social movements would be better off putting their energy elsewhere; relying on the state to validate claims constrains the possibility of radical social change. Others hold more tempered views, acknowledging that legal strategies can spur activism even when they fail to achieve stated goals. According to this view, law and social movements are mutually constitutive, but legal mobilization does not go far enough in understanding the relationship between law and society.

Today, as LGBTQ and other legal protections hang in the balance, we ought to move beyond the narrow question of the generic benefit or harm of legal strategies. We need a broader focus, in particular, on the interplay among law, social movements, and institutions. Rather than view the law in isolation from the rest of society, we must recognize that law has a complex relationship with other social and cultural institutions and that legal strategies do not represent the totality of social movement activism.

Indeed, the law is inextricably linked to systems of cultural meaning—systems comprised of what sociologist Ann Swidler has called a "cultural toolkit" consisting of narratives, images, and discourse that help to make sense of the world. In the case of sexual orientation and gender identity, an overlapping network of institutions—religion, psychiatry, and the law itself—has been particularly powerful in shaping the lives of LGBTQ people, having variously defined them as sinners, disordered, or criminals. Even where they have been marked by internal disagreement over priorities, LGBTQ social movements have had great success over the last few decades in challenging these institutional configurations.

What does this mean for LGBTQ people today? The bevy of new legislative efforts by the right looks, in effect, like an attempt to pretend, if not quite pray, the gay and trans away. In an ironic display of the so-called cancel culture that they claim to oppose, Republicans are intent on disappearing LGBTQ people under the guise of protecting children—never mind that many of these children may be queer themselves or have queer parents, relatives, and friends. Legal advances won in recent years may be at risk not because of bigotry toward LGBTQ people, but because of electoral advantages that reward a vocal minority of right-wing politicians. These same politicians strategically wield anti-LGBTQ proposals as wedge issues to propel social conservatives—especially white evangelicals—to the polls. Any analysis of the relationship between the law and progressive social movements must take such structural power into account, but it must also contend with the complex, dialectical interplay between legal and social change.

AN IMPORTANT CASE STUDY is the history of the fight for same-sex marriage. Though activists have long debated the role that marriage equality should play—some view it as oppressive in its own right, while others argue it is simply not the most important issue facing LGBTQ communities—large swaths of LGBTQ people mobilized to achieve same-sex marriage. Skeptics note that focusing on the legal demand for marriage recognition diverted time, resources, and energy away from broader social and political change, constricted political imagination, or even defused more radical transformation. But legal strategies are only one part of the broader LGBTQ movement. Underlying the marriage equality victory were decades of organized and individual struggles—sometimes unified, sometimes at odds—to gain social, economic, and legal support for LGBTQ people and their families. These efforts created widespread institutional change that will be hard to undo, even as their precise significance and implications continue to be debated within the LGBTQ community.

To take one example, employee resource groups placed pressure on corporate employers to advocate for same-sex marriage.

While corporations had their own interests, such as streamlining how they distribute benefits, such groups contributed to changing corporate policies. Many Fortune 500 companies, for example, enacted domestic partner policies before same-sex marriage was legally recognized by the state. This pressure came from both inside and outside. Employee resource groups pushed companies to change their policies, and outside groups such as the Human Rights Campaign began to rank companies based on their Corporate Equality Index. Still more radical groups such as ACT UP threatened to protest companies they deemed homophobic, enabling the employee groups, which looked tamer by comparison, to exert greater leverage.

One significant result of this activism came in 2015, when a group called 379 Employers and Organizations Representing Employers, including Fortune 100 companies and small businesses, filed an amicus brief in *Obergefell* supporting marriage equality. A coalition of large labor unions including the AFL-CIO, Change to Win, and the National Education Association together representing nearly 20 million workers also filed an amicus brief in favor of marriage equality, the outcome of internal pressure for change. While religious opposition to same-sex marriage continues, especially among Catholic and evangelical organizations, there were also three different briefs submitted by other religious groups, including Quakers and another representing an array of individual clergy, religious groups, and organizations. Finally, the American Psychological Association and the American Public Health Association along with Whitman-Walker Health each filed a brief in support of same-sex marriage.

These briefs are significant not only because of their arguments, or because of the wide range of popular support from very different social domains that they marshalled on behalf of same-sex marriage, but also because they are products of a vast network of unseen and far-reaching social movement activism. Some of this activism is largely invisible to the public, taking place slowly over decades within corporate conference rooms, as in the case of employee resource groups. Other efforts are more public, such as that of the HRC and ACT UP. The HRC continues to use reputational threat and incentives to cajole companies to adopt a greater array of LGBTQ-friendly policies and practices, such as educating employees about appropriate use of pronouns with coworkers and customers and providing gender-affirming care to employees.

Psychology and psychiatry have also wielded great power over what today we refer to as LGBTQ communities. Lesbians and gay men had once been subject to abusive efforts to "cure" them that ranged from the now discredited "conversion" or "reparative" therapy to barbaric electroshock treatments. Beginning with its first edition in 1952, homosexuality was listed as a psychiatric disorder in the *Diagnostic and Statistical Manual of Mental Disorders* published by the American Psychiatric Association (APA), severely impeding efforts to win equal rights and equal treatment before the law. But after decades of sustained, multi-pronged activism, the APA removed homosexuality from its list of mental disorders in 1973 and adopted resolutions deploring discrimination against "homosexuals" in housing, employment, and licensing and demanding that the government repeal anti-sodomy statutes.

This shift—a victory of social movement activism—took place outside the law, but it had a profound impact on broader cultural norms and public opinion, which in turn shaped new legal changes and protections. LGBTQ activists demanded that researchers conduct controlled studies of noninstitutionalized populations of straight and gay people rather than relying on homophobic assumptions. New studies found gay and straight groups indistinguishable from each other in blind controlled studies, upending the view that lesbians and gay men suffered from mental illness. This effort, along with protests, challenged the cultural logic and categories of an institution with great power to regulate and discipline LGBTQ people. In turn, LGBTQ activists had a new tool they could bring to bear on the state when demanding changes in laws and policies.

For example, the National Gay Task Force (now the National LGBTQ Task Force), together with the APA, the American Psychological Association, and the American Public Health Association and Health Service, all took part in lobbying the U.S. Public Health Service to change its classification of homosexuality from a mental illness in the late 1970s. The Immigration and Naturalization Service relied on the U.S. Public Health Service's diagnosis to deny citizenship to lesbian and gay aliens. Court decisions in 1977 resulted in a new policy that no longer viewed homosexuality as an inherent index of "poor moral character." The following year, the U.S. Public Health Service adopted the APA's decision that homosexuality was not a pathology. While removing the equation of homosexuality with pathology that had provided a categorical barrier to citizenship for gay and lesbian people did not eliminate all obstacles for lesbian and gay immigrants, it changed the terms of the debate and marked an important cultural shift that would shape future immigration and citizenship policy.

This is just one of many examples of leveraging one institution to affect change in another. Activists continue to challenge how the APA diagnoses and handles the care of people who are transgender or have intersex traits. While support of trans children varies greatly across the country, the move has been in the general direction of providing gender-affirming care, though of course we are far from there yet. Intersex advocacy groups continue to challenge the medical community for performing medically unnecessary surgeries on infants born with intersex traits across the world.

MEMBERSHIP IN WHAT cultural anthropologist Gayle Rubin calls the "charmed circle" of social acceptance is always provisional, and the latest attempts to marginalize and exile LGBTQ people from full and equal citizenship are a case in point. How these efforts will play out in the short term remains to be seen, but what is clear is that to understand the current political moment for LGBTQ people, we need a more nuanced view of law's place in society. The law is subject to its own internal logic and to the pendulum swings of electoral circumstance, but it cannot be divorced from its wider social, cultural, and institutional context.

Bernstein

On the one hand, this means that the law is far too often a tool of the powerful who benefit from structural inequalities. On the other hand, the embeddedness of law in society also makes it a resource for the marginalized and sensitive to the many other institutions that shape our social life. At the end of the day, profound cultural shifts and institutional changes in the United States over the last several decades will ensure that these latest efforts to legislate anti-LGBTQ prejudice remain vigorously contested at all levels of society, from the halls of formal political power to medical associations and protests organized by young people. Gay and trans people can't and won't be legislated away. In the meantime, we must work to oppose the harm that has already been done and is still being perpetrated by dangerous rhetoric and the laws that have already made it onto the books. Doing so will require both tactical and strategic pluralism, marshalling legal challenges and electoral mobilization as well as the rich legacy of social movement activism that LGBTQ people and their allies have to draw on.

RETHINKING HUMAN RIGHTS
Zachary Manfredi

IN 2017 Senator Bernie Sanders made the Republicans' tax bill a human rights issue by connecting it to UN Special Rapporteur Philip Alston's investigation of "extreme poverty" in the United States. Following a meeting with Sanders, Alston castigated the legislation for its potential to exacerbate already historic levels of economic inequality and social immiseration. "Tax policy is human rights policy," Alston had declared, and the Republican bill represented "America's bid to become the most unequal society in the world." In the wake of the finalization of the tax law—arguably one of the greatest tax transfers of wealth to the rich in modern times—activists took up this framing, decrying the human rights implications of the law in creating radical economic disparities.

In the years since the Trump tax legislation took effect, major progressive political figures in the United States have continued to draw rhetorical connections among tax policy, extreme inequality, and human rights. Throughout his 2020 primary campaign, Sanders offered proposals to guarantee housing, medical care, and education "as human rights" and explicitly tied funding of these novel social programs to a wealth tax. Senator Elizabeth Warren and Representative Pramila Jayapal have similarly introduced the Ultra-Millionaire Tax Act aimed at providing funding for public services. And Representative Alexandria Ocasio-Cortez has called for the United States to ratify the International Covenant on Economic, Social, and Cultural Rights as part of her legislative package for "A Just Society." In making the case for legislative proposals addressing housing justice, immigrant and workers' rights, and the federal poverty line, Ocasio-Cortez has frequently framed progressive taxation policy as a means to fund programs that would guarantee the rights elaborated in the covenant.

What is at stake in couching these visions of tax policy—a domain often sealed off from larger debates about values—in the language of human rights? On the one hand, it might be thought to deepen the appeal of progressive political programs by highlighting how they aim to improve the basic economic, social, and political needs of their constituents. On the other hand, even as major figures on the U.S. political left mount such arguments, recent critical commentary on human rights evinces a longstanding tradition of skepticism about human rights' emancipatory potential. Some scholars argue that the simultaneous ascendancy of human rights advocacy and neoliberal governance since the 1970s is far from coincidental and trace how neoliberal reformers often relied upon the language of human rights and its affinity with the self-interested, consumerist individual. Others criticize human rights advocacy for its minimalist vision and lament its compatibility with radical inequality.

Although this legacy of left skepticism about human rights retains valuable lessons for advocates, our political moment also provides opportunities for the reconceptualization and radicalization of human rights programs. Contemporary appeals to human rights arguably have the most to offer by developing a more egalitarian dimension to the politics of human rights. The traditional liberal conception of human rights as individual entitlements limits the capacity of the state to regulate private power and mobilizes state authority on behalf of private property and capital accumulation. By contrast, progressive appeals to human rights can link this language to a normative vision for a more just social order and the provision of public welfare. Developing an egalitarian vision requires moving beyond a guarantee of sufficient minimums and instead emphasizing how radical social and economic inequality stifle the realization of a more robust and radical human rights project.

SINCE AT LEAST Karl Marx's famous 1844 commentary on the French Declaration of the Rights of Man and of the Citizen, many left thinkers have been suspicious of the conceptual foundation and practical implications of human rights. As Marx saw it, the declaration underwrote a regime of private property that stifled "genuine human emancipation" while simultaneously absolving the state from addressing social and economic domination in the sphere of "civil society." On this account, just as the state proclaims the formal equality of all persons, it simultaneously abdicates responsibility for private forms of discrimination and social domination. (Rights to private property and free trade offer no comfort to those without food, shelter, or housing.) Worse still, the imagined subject of rights was, for Marx, nothing other than the self-interested "egoistic" bourgeois whose "liberty" to engage in trade, contract, and property acquisition would be secured at precisely the same time that the social and communal aspects of human social life would be denied.

More generally, critics have long observed that a narrow focus on "rights talk" and formal equality can obscure and even ratify substantive inequalities. Early writings of the Critical Legal Studies movement, for example, contended that the promulgation of legal rights can exacerbate conditions of oppression. In their edited volume *Left Legalism/Left Critique* (2002), political theorist Wendy Brown and legal scholar Janet Halley noted that "for all the content they may be given by their location in liberal orders," rights "retain a certain formality and emptiness which allow them to be deployed and redeployed by different political contestants"— including those staunchly opposed to economic redistribution. In similar fashion, contemporary scholars observe how rights claims are invoked to prevent the redistributive taxation of privately held capital, to protect the rights of corporate entities to "speak" as in *Citizens United*, and to weaken the power of labor unions with "right to work" laws. In his recent book *How Rights Went Wrong: Why Our Obsession with Rights Is Tearing America Apart* (2021), legal scholar Jamal Greene laments how "American courts draw firm lines, often in morally arbitrary ways, between the interests they consider rights and those they don't."

Two contemporary trends in the left criticism of human rights are particularly notable. First, historian Samuel Moyn has argued that human rights advocacy has, in practice, been limited to a minimalist agenda that remains indifferent to the development of extreme inequality. On this account, human rights movements have focused on only the most extreme abuses of state violence and—at best—contemplated guaranteeing a set of minimal social and economic "floor conditions." "Even perfectly realized human rights are compatible with radical inequality," Moyn argues. As a result of their indifference to inequality, Moyn despairs that human rights movements and legal regimes proved to be "helpless bystanders of market fundamentalism."

Second, other critics have observed an essential affinity between human rights projects and neoliberalism. Decades ago, anthropologist Talal Asad suggested that "the historical convergence of human rights and neoliberalism may not be purely accidental," since human rights notions of "self-ownership" and "self-preservation" align with neoliberal economics' understanding of human beings as pieces of "human capital" always striving for greater self-augmentation. Critics worry that the legal protections offered by a theory of human rights predicated on a consumerist subject will focus primarily on creation of "free markets" and justify policies that intensify social and economic stratification. Left critics of human rights also observe that different rights regimes encourage and produce particular self-conception among rights holders: if a human right to private property or wealth accumulation is enshrined in law, it helps establish a framework for how people evaluate their life projects.

Recent work by Jessica Whyte and Quinn Slobodian advances this argument and showcases how neoliberal reformers often relied on the language of human rights as part of their own political programs. In *Globalists: The End of Empire and Birth of Neoliberalism* (2018), Slobodian shows how Geneva School neoliberals who were instrumental in the development of postwar international institutions—such as Ludwig von Mises, Fredrich Hayek, and Wilhelm Röpke—framed human rights as "xenos rights," that is, rights of security for foreign capital and protections of private property against state expropriation. In addition, Whyte's 2019 book *The Morals of Market: Human Rights and the Rise of Neoliberalism* shows how "neoliberals developed their own account of human rights as moral and legal supports for a liberal market order." As Whyte documents, neoliberals relied on human rights to advance a consumerist vision of the welfare state subject to means-testing and compatible with international human rights instruments. They appealed to human rights as reason to oppose postcolonial projects of economic redistribution and industry nationalization, including notably opposition to the New International Economic Order. And they turned to human rights as justification for radical programs of reform in Chile and elsewhere that focused on privatization, deregulation of financial markets, and destruction of labor unions.

Taking these critiques seriously raises the concern that contemporary progressive appeals to human rights—even if they result in formal recognition of new rights—may prove ineffectual at achieving meaningful social transformation or even actively obstructionist or distracting. Might a narrow focus on securing human rights result in a limited set of reforms to secure minimal sets of goods for the worst-off, while remaining indifferent to the pernicious effects of radical economic inequalities? Or, perhaps worse yet, does the framing of progressive policy goals in terms of human rights leave those programs open to easy cooptation by neoliberal reformers who see human rights as compatible with their own vision of market fundamentalism?

WE SHOULD NOT DENY the purchase of these critiques, but it is important to see what is potentially distinctive about new appeals to human rights as part of progressive policy. For one thing, the growing contemporary focus on the social and economic dimensions of human rights already helps recast them in ways that depart from neoliberal formulations. We should take the occasion of progressive appeals to human rights as an opportunity for rights' reinvention—for explaining why, in the context of progressive advocacy, human rights ought to entail a more egalitarian and redistributive political program.

In fact, the tax focus of Jayapal, Bernie Sanders, Elizabeth Warren, Alexandria Ocasio-Cortez, and others is part of a broader progressive shift toward taking social and economic rights seriously. In the wake of both the 2008 global financial crisis and the ascendance of far-right political forces, across the left political spectrum different actors have increasingly emphasized the significance of social and economic rights as a means of addressing widespread social turmoil. Progressives now regularly refer to health care, housing, and education as human rights. Sanders, for example, has explicitly called for a "21st Century Economic Bill of Rights," which would establish a living wage, quality health care, complete education, affordable housing, clean environment, and secure retirement as human rights. These political invocations of social and economic rights owe much to the work of social movements. From the early days of the Occupy assemblies to the rhetoric of Black Lives Matter leaders, post–financial crisis social movements within the United States have turned to the language of human rights to make demands for domestic social and political transformation.

As Alston's case makes clear, a turn to social and economic rights has also been witnessed at the level of more traditional international human rights institutions over the past decade. In a June 2016 address to the UN's Human Rights Council, Alston underscored that UN human rights organs and transnational NGOs had historically treated economic and social rights, in particular, as "marginal." Alston shares with human rights skeptics a deep concern about how inequality within states has intensified under conditions of economic globalization, financial market deregulation, and trade liberalization since the 1970s. As he put it in 2016, "the winds of globalization are blowing in directions that are not at all favourable to" economic and social rights. Alston's far-reaching work with the United Nations between 2014 and 2020 helped reorient human rights advocacy toward social and economic rights in such domains as tax policy, financial regulation, social welfare protections, antidiscrimination, and universal basic income. This project might thus be read as acknowledging some core insights of human rights skepticism while attempting to rectify the failings of human rights through a revitalizing of existing legal instruments such as the International Labour Organization's Indigenous and Tribal Peoples Convention and the International Convention on the Elimination of Forms of Racial Discrimination. In these cases, Alston aims to show how existing human rights could be interpreted to necessitate more aggressive political programs of redistribution.

In this regard it seems essential to note that in some respects, the substantive content of rights claims championed by recent progressive political actors differ dramatically from the rights preferred by neoliberal reformers. Human rights to education, housing, protection from racial discrimination, gender equality, union membership, sustenance, and water all emerged over the course of the twentieth century, and new rights instruments and declarations were often developed in response to the demands of left social movements. As scholars such as Stefan-Ludwig Hoffmann have documented, the history of international human rights law is complex and polyvalent: within the twentieth century alone, socialist, postcolonial, and other left critics of neoliberalism have, at times, relied on human rights as part of their own vocabularies of justice. From Ernst Bloch's arguments that only socialism could properly realize the promise of human rights to Malcolm X's claim that human rights were a superior alternative to civil rights for holding Western governments accountable for the legacy of racism, numerous radical thinkers have relied on the language of human rights. In this sense, the progressive turn to a more robust vision of social and economic rights language might be seen as an attempt to resuscitate a more radical tradition of human rights advocacy as an alternative to mainstream liberal and neoliberal formations. This work requires recognizing the plasticity of law and its potential to develop in new directions. This does not mean we should fall prey to what international law scholar Susan Marks has called "false contingency" regarding rights—that is, the assumption that human rights are infinitely malleable and repurposable for left politics. But in the twenty-first-century context of extreme economic inequality, claims that there are human rights to food, water, nondiscrimination, housing, and labor protections may prove more protean and radical than previously imagined.

Even granting these possibilities, however, it isn't obvious that simply focusing on social and economic rights responds to the most fundamental insights of left critiques. Consider first the objection that, even when successfully enshrined in law and ensured by states, human rights set minimums but largely ignore radical economic inequality per se by attending more to conditions of absolute material deprivation and oppression rather than the relative disparities in power. Perhaps a right to adequate housing for all still says little about the apparent injustice of a social order where millions live in meager one-room homes while a class of billionaires occupies mansions. We might query whether human rights only speak to distributive justice as a matter of contingency: When basic social and economic rights are not protected in a social order with vast disparities in wealth, do human rights principles only demand that redistribution occur to the point where rights are minimally satisfied? Worse yet, do rights claims then risk serving as an apology for a "minimalist justice" that could blunt demands for more radical social transformation? And if progressive appeals to human rights remain confined in this way, are they really so incompatible with the neoliberal vision of rights that can justify programs of privatization and deregulation?

In this sense, critiques of human rights call our attention to the importance of developing a more radically egalitarian vision of human rights advocacy. Egalitarianism, in this sense, should not be construed as merely a matter of formal equality before the law: the insistence, say, that all members of a polity have "equal rights" in the sense of equal claim to a minimal set of rights claims. Rather, a genuinely egalitarian politics of human rights should underscore the ways that radical social, economic, and political inequality necessarily enable widespread violations of human rights. This is not only because, practically speaking, the concentration of private wealth makes it difficult to achieve even the minimum guarantees of basic economic and social rights. Extreme inequalities in wealth also create disparities in political power and fundamentally undermine democratic control over economic governance. Radical inequality thus undermines human rights because it stifles even the basic right to equal say in the democratic political process that ought to determine what social and economic orders reign.

Consider, for instance, how human rights advocates have argued that the "interconnectedness" of different kinds of human rights necessarily implicates inequality. In a 2016 address, Alston invoked the 1993 Vienna Declaration to make this point: "all human rights are universal, indivisible and interdependent and interrelated. The international community must treat human rights globally in a fair and equal manner, on the same footing, and with the same emphasis."

Manfredi

A recurrent theme of Alston's work is that inequality and extreme poverty impair one's ability to enjoy almost all human rights. In this sense, it can be cast as a revival of arguments associated with traditions of socialist political theory and welfare liberalism that view material well-being as a prerequisite for active participation in political life. In the United States, this tradition draws inspiration from Franklin D. Roosevelt's call in 1944 for a "second Bill of Rights under which a new basis of security and prosperity can be established for all" and its role as an antecedent to various articulations of welfarism.

Writers in these traditions have long underscored that conditions of economic precarity—for instance, lack of reliable access to housing, food, water, or medical care—can make political participation and cultural expression nearly impossible. In this regard, we might develop Alston's arguments about interconnectedness further and insist that extreme forms of inequality are in themselves antithetical to human rights: when material disparities in economic and social resources are substantial, the economically powerful may prevent others from exercising political and civil rights as well. At the very least, this argument suggests that both theorists and advocates ought to reassess the multiple dimensions on which inequality implicates human rights.

Recent progressive takes on tax policy are particularly interesting examples of how one might develop such an egalitarian account of human rights. As a matter of political rhetoric, progressive politicians have framed their tax proposals specifically as a reaction to both insufficient minimums and to radical economic inequality. Moreover, in a substantial sense these programs have an inherently egalitarian dimension: reducing the holdings of the wealthiest (while either not decreasing or increasing the wealth of those with fewer resources) reduces economic inequality. Framing progressive taxation as a human rights issue then implies an affinity between realizing human rights and securing a more egalitarian social order.

More specifically, one might think of the egalitarian connection between human rights and progressive tax policy along three dimensions.

First, and most obviously, progressives argue that taxation can enable the provision of social goods that create a more egalitarian society. If rights to health care, education, housing, and a clean environment entail such social programs as universal health care, affordable housing, and equitable public education (both K–12 and postsecondary), then they also entail a robustly egalitarian tax policy. The progressive vision for these programs entails far more than providing minimums for the worst-off: more fundamentally, by providing robust public alternatives to private provision of essential goods, progressive policies challenge the market-driven approach of neoliberal political economy.

Second, progressive tax policy is egalitarian because it can lessen disparities in political power. In line with Alston's discussion of the "interconnectedness" of human rights, progressive tax policy focusing on eliminating extreme wealth disparities may limit the ability of the extremely wealthy to exercise influence over politics. If campaign finance laws once aimed at creating an equal playing field, so too can limiting the overall wealth of individuals curtail political influence. Progressive tax policies and other programs that restrict "dark money," eliminate politicians' ability to trade stocks, and limit corporate funding of political campaigns all aim to prevent powerful actors from crowding out other voices. In this sense, progressive tax policy supports an egalitarian vision of human rights along the lines of the expansive articulation of the interconnectedness thesis: policies that curb the influence of the economically powerful allow for a more egalitarian exercise of political and civil rights.

Third, an egalitarian account of human rights clarifies how conservative and neoliberal tax policy leads to human rights violations. Consider how advocacy along these lines might have taken shape if applied to the 2018 Trump tax legislation. Framing different features of the law as a "human rights" violations can illuminate some of their most pernicious dimensions: the initial House bill's tax of graduate students "ghost tuition" could have been framed as an attack on the human right to education by depriving all but the wealthiest of access to graduate degrees; the repeal of the ACA individual mandate was in fact framed by some as a violation of the human right to health care; and the elimination of state tax deductions could have been articulated as an assault on the human right to housing. When framed as human rights violations, arcane and technical tax proposals appear politically salient and imperative. A human rights analysis, in short, highlights how law and policy implicate fundamental freedoms and human needs.

ALTHOUGH THIS ANALYSIS offers only a cursory outline of possible lines of argument, it suggests what might also be gained by linking progressive policy programs to egalitarian accounts of human rights. Against the backdrop of rising far-right political forces, social disintegration, and inequities laid bare by the pandemic years, progressive political actors and social movements concerned about inequality are engaged in evolving practices of advocacy, experimentation, and dissident protest. In the United States, in particular, a vast array of political energies and institutional resources that previously supported "international" human rights movements now increasingly find their attention focused on domestic abuses of human rights. The convergence of these energies with renewed focuses on progressive economic and social policy may yet provide new opportunities—both theoretical and strategic—for egalitarian advocates to realize a more robust vision of human rights.

LAW FOR BLACK RADICAL LIBERATION
Paul Gowder

IN 1860 Frederick Douglass was in exile in Glasgow to avoid arrest in connection with John Brown's raid on Harpers Ferry. No stranger to revolutionary tactics, Douglass had long known Brown and was accused of being a coconspirator in the raid; after his return to the United States, Douglass even gave a speech in support of Brown. But during his exile, at an event before the Scottish Anti-Slavery Society, he had a different subject: a defense of the potential of the Constitution. In his address, Douglass didn't contest how the Constitution had been crafted and interpreted to protect the institution of slavery. Nonetheless, he argued that the document had antislavery implications—and, in particular, that "the Constitution will afford slavery no protection when it shall cease to be administered by slaveholders." Contrary to the followers of William Lloyd Garrison, who understood the Constitution as an ineluctably proslavery document and thought that the dissolution of the Union would be necessary to end slavery, the way forward, as Douglass saw it, was to "vote such men into power as will use their powers for the abolition of slavery."

While much of Douglass's argument hinged on specific constitutional provisions that were inconsistent with slavery and with the legal regime put in place to support it—the Fifth Amendment's Due Process Clause being the most obvious—it also relied on a claim about the nature of law itself. "Law is not merely an arbitrary enactment with regard to justice, reason, or humanity," Douglass said. He went on:

> There must be something more than history—something more than tradition. . . . There is another rule of law. . . . Where a law is susceptible of two meanings, the one making it accomplish an innocent purpose, and the other making it accomplish a wicked purpose, we must in all cases adopt that which makes it accomplish an innocent purpose.

As a matter of legal methodology, Douglass was quite right. There is a long tradition in Anglo-American and Commonwealth courts of deploying aggressively narrow judicial interpretation of positive enactments of law in order to preserve an underlying conception of fundamental legality. David Dyzenhaus, for example, has documented the power of common law courts even in systems of parliamentary supremacy to narrowly interpret privative clauses—those that strip individuals of the right of access to courts—in the interests of more fundamental ideas of legal order. The Fugitive Slave Act of 1850 was itself a privative clause that stripped allegedly escaped slaves of judicial protections with which they might defend their freedom.

Gowder

More broadly, Douglass recognized what we might call the entrepreneurial potential of the law. Because law tends to make its claims in universalistic terms, it provides the intellectual material to ground the demand for inclusion. In the case of the United States, which had in fact deployed the rhetoric of universal rights since its inception, Douglass's argument amounted to saying: the Constitution does prohibit these forms of oppression—and if you took it seriously, you'd enforce those prohibitions. And in making this argument he could appeal to the universality of law itself, along with a methodological tradition that supported it.

Douglass's view has been a perennial touchstone in debates about the Constitution, but it is worth revisiting for another reason, as well. In the political sphere, both scholars and activists involved in movements for social justice have often questioned whether a focus on law and on legal rights promotes individualistic remedies over group solidarity. On this point, Douglass's argument—and the history of Black liberation movements more broadly—reveals how the language of the law can be a basis for collective demands. While skeptics are right to observe that legal victories alone tend to be unstable, the same can be said about other forms of social transformation—as historian David Waldstreicher recently noted in these pages, even "revolutions aren't all they're sometimes cracked up to be"—and there is a rich tradition showing how legal and political efforts can reinforce rather than undermine one another. At a moment in which both the rule of law and the progress toward racial and social justice of the last half-century in the United States appear to be under severe threat, this history shows how the law can remain an essential resource in building a more just world.

DOUGLASS'S BELIEF in the emancipatory potential of law—at least in the hands of organized political movements—resonates with socialist historian E. P. Thompson's defense of the rule of law in *Whigs and Hunters: The Origin of the Black Act* (1975), a study of the legal conflict over rights to forests in eighteenth-century England. Though best known as the pioneering social historian of *The Making of the English Working Class* (1963), Thompson also contributed to the development of what might be called *left legalism*. Addressing structuralist Marxists such as French philosopher Louis Althusser, who were skeptical of law's relation to capitalism, Thompson argued that the very ideological function of law—its layering a veneer of universal justice over capitalist power relations—in fact rendered it useful to movements for justice. "In a context of gross class inequalities," Thompson concedes, "the equity of the law must always be in some part sham." Yet even in the case of the law of British imperialism, "the rules and the rhetoric have imposed some inhibitions upon the imperial power. If the rhetoric was a mask, it was a mask which Gandhi and Nehru were to borrow, at the head of a million masked supporters." In short, the law provided a rhetorical framework for revolutionary demands in the form of universal legal rights.

This subversive capacity of law arguably rests on three distinctive features, at least within the Anglo-American common law tradition.

The first is as Thompson identified it: the law makes its appeal in terms of universal principles and (particularly in liberal democracies) underlying universal values. Such societies, as Moses Finley explains in his 1971 lecture "The Ancestral Constitution," tend to tell valorizing stories about their founders and the ideals which they imbued their institutions. It is with regard to these kinds of features that legal scholar Tomiko Brown-Nagin has written of "law as a cultural resource." Campaigns against police brutality from the 1960s through the present Movement for Black Lives have "invoked the national commitment to the rule of law and equal protection" in an effort to "demonstrate hypocrisy by the state or its agents" with the goal of gaining "public recognition and credibility," Brown-Nagin notes. The tactic of using law to identify and resist the hypocrisy of the powerful can be observed in the practical implementation of law as well—in particular, the legal technique of appealing to precedent. By dint of law's universality, a rule applied in one case ought to be applied in another. Combining this with the logic of precedent, the extension of rights to one person can serve as a foundation for the extension of rights to others.

Second, the individualized nature of adjudication—as well as the way that appeals to precedent require comparisons across different cases—forces a kind of recognition of shared humanity. Skilled lawyers recognize that the trial is a setting for narrative, in which the interests and characters of those whose behavior are at issue are put on display and organized into a story that will be recognizable—because of the way that the characters in the trial are shown to respond to universal human motives—to juries and judges and the communities at large. In her book *Double Character: Slavery and Mastery in the Antebellum Southern Courtroom* (2000), for example, historian Ariela Gross shows that the process of applying legal methods to the behavior of enslaved people served a humanizing function at odds with the views of enslavers—embedding into legal doctrine the fact that enslaved people were indeed people, rather than mere property.

Third, to the extent the law offers any constraints on governments and powerful interests, the enforcement of those constraints requires at least the credible threat of coordinated action by ordinary people, even if only by those privileged enough to enjoy the benefits of legal protection. But the need to recruit ordinary people into the law's defense has significant consequences for campaigns for freedom and equality. For example, it assumes the existence of robust civil society institutions among those who benefit from the law. Of course, such institutions may be vulnerable to copying or outright joining by the subordinated: antebellum Black Americans organized their own churches and Freemason lodges, effectively creating their own civil society out of preexisting forms that whites deployed. Moreover, shifting power balances may well require that the privileged recruit the subordinated to help enforce their legal rights. That, in turn, requires that the substance of the law is, or can be, sufficiently to their advantage to motivate their participation.

These features of law may help explain why Black liberation activists have so often appealed to the law and the idea of individual rights protected by law. They have done so in both subversive and solidarity-building ways, sometimes both at the same time.

A striking example comes from Black Panthers Bobby Seale and Huey Newton. In his book *Seize the Time: The Story of the Black Panther Party* (1970), Seale recounts a confrontation between Newton and the police over a demand to search a car full of guns. When Newton vigorously appeals to his constitutional rights, he appears to confound the police, who were clearly used to seeing the Constitution as the patriotic fount of their own authority. He then threatens to back up his appeal to law with an appeal to arms. "When the pig says, 'You're just turning the Constitution around,' Huey says, 'I'm turning nothing around. I'm exercising my constitutional right. I've got the gun to back it up!'" While the threat of violence was of course a key part of this confrontation, the universality of the law and the difficulty of openly saying that it protected police but not Black citizens played an inextricable role in supporting Newton's resistance. His appeal to law also gave courage to observers, some of whom would later join the movement:

> 'Don't go anywhere! These pigs can't keep you from observing. You have a right to observe an officer carrying out his duty.' And these pigs, they listened to this shit. See, Huey's citing law and shit.

Newton thus used the law to keep the police from responding effectively to his armed resistance and to prevent them from dispersing his audience. His audience, in turn, was inspired by his capacity to resist a small army of police, a foundational move in the Black Panthers' effort to build a force to protect their community from police violence: "After *that*," Seale writes, "we really began to patrol pigs then, because we got righteous recruits."

The Newton confrontation, like Douglass's speech, tracks Thompson's and Brown-Nagin's account of how law can be used by social movements. Moreover, the way that Newton's invocation of law confounded the police serves as a vivid illustration of Thompson's claim that a ruling class can be trapped by its own habit of using law to support its own interests. It was precisely because the Oakland police viewed the law as the normative foundation of their own authority—precisely because it offered the rhetorical terrain in which they tended to win conflicts—that the officers were vulnerable to Newton's tactic.

Newton fit his appeal to law into his broader movement goals by using the power of law as a recruiting tool. But the universality of law can also serve as a direct element of a political appeal by movement organizations. In 1838, for example, a committee of Black Pennsylvanians met to organize resistance to a new state constitution that would have stripped them of the right to vote. They released a broadside, "Appeal of Forty Thousand Citizens, Threatened with Disenfranchisement, to the People of Pennsylvania," which emphasized two ideas. First, they argued that disenfranchising Black Pennsylvanians would make everyone's rights less secure. "It is the safeguard of the strongest that he lives under a government which is obliged to respect the voice of the weakest," they wrote. They also predicted that taking away their right to vote would undermine their incentive to participate in all kinds of collective projects: it would "starve our patriotism" and "turn into gall and wormwood the friendship we bear to yourselves." Second, they argued that Black Pennsylvanians were the same in all relevant respects as whites: they had been considered citizens at the time of the state's founding, they paid taxes, they were working and productive members of society, and they had served along with whites in the Revolutionary War.

In one particularly interesting passage, the appeal responds to white objections that permitting them the vote would promote "intermixture of the races":

> Then let the indentures, title-deeds, contracts, notes of hand, and all other evidences of bargain, in which colored men have been treated as men, be torn and scattered on the winds. Consistency is a jewel. Let no white man hereafter ask his colored neighbor's consent when he wants his property or his labor, lest he should endanger the Anglo-Saxon purity of his descendants? Why should not the same principle hold good between neighbor and neighbor, which is deemed necessary, as a fundamental principle, in the Constitution itself?

In its appeal to "consistency," this passage is a sort of apotheosis of liberal legalism: it points to Black–white parity in market transactions as the basis for a parallel claim about political transactions. Yet, despite its capitalist and individualistic foundation, the actual use to which this claim is put isn't an individual's appeal for some kind of right to property but rather a liberation movement's appeal for the democratic right to vote to pursue shared ends.

LIKE DOUGLASS, the Panthers and the Pennsylvanians challenge the presumption that law is essentially individualistic—that it "ratifies and legitimates an adversarial, competitive, and atomistic conception of human relations," as legal historian Morton J. Horwitz has put it—and that in virtue of its individualism it impedes efforts at political organizing. History reveals that law can play a much different role, one focused less on individual litigation or the belief that enlightened judges will save the oppressed and more on collective political action—and yet still be distinctively legal. Douglass recognized that the law could be turned into a force for good in the hands of "abolition statesmen"—that is, as the product of political action that made use of the distinctive and useful tools that law offers. The Panthers recognized that even abusive cops had been conditioned to take appeals to law seriously and used that knowledge to confound police misconduct and inspire acts of organized resistance. And the Pennsylvanians recognized that the logic of the law could be put to service in explaining their claims to full political agency in the first place.

This is not to deny that even successful efforts to use law to promote social progress risk reinforcing unjust power relations. In an unjust society, the law is bound to be double-faced. Consider what I have elsewhere called the "paradox of property" in U.S. law. On the one hand, property rights laid the legal foundation for slavery. (Indeed, the contention that enslaved people were "property" was the only legal argument enslavers had for the persistence and enforcement of their supposed legal rights over the enslaved.) The U.S. legal order's property defense of slavery reached a peak in *Dred Scott v. Sandford* (1857), which struck down the Missouri Compromise on the grounds that Congress's prohibition of slavery in the territories would deprive enslavers of their property. On the other hand, the conception of property embedded in this terrible legacy would ultimately be put to use as part of a campaign for

Black inclusion. A century after *Dred Scott*, the Black-led National Welfare Rights Organization and the lawyers inspired by it scored a significant victory in *Goldberg v. Kelly* (1970), which expanded the constitutional conception of property in order to provide legal protections to recipients of certain government entitlements.

One might reasonably inquire about the price of such victories. To what extent, for example, did the manipulation of the concepts of property and entitlement to encompass welfare rights divert attention from challenges to the underlying economic inequality that made welfare necessary in the first place? Is the very enterprise of litigating on behalf of the rights of the poor "enmeshed in a social system—the attorney/client relation—consigning the poor to the status of dependent other," as Anthony Alfieri has argued?

Again and again the record appears ambivalent. In 1866 Douglass's vision of an abolitionist Constitution was achieved in the Fourteenth Amendment and its equal protection clause. It took another century and another victory in *Brown v. Board of Education* before desegregation efforts were implemented, and even that legacy is questionable. Yet still the Fourteenth Amendment was useful to Black freedom movements before *Brown*. Historians such as Megan Ming Francis and Michael Klarman have observed that the early criminal justice reforms of the Warren Court—including efforts to prevent coerced confessions and make the constitutional right to counsel real and effective—have their origins in the anti-lynching movement. After the NAACP's efforts to obtain action against lynching in Congress and the White House failed, they turned to the courts, and—making use of the "incorporation" idea that the Fourteenth Amendment applied the criminal procedure protections of the Constitution to the states—won a number of early battles that both undermined lynch law and built some of the foundational precedent for the more robust rights that today's criminal defendants still enjoy.

These victories seem equivocal at best. The constitutional criminal justice revolution of the mid-twentieth century may have established substantial formal rights for defendants, but the criminal justice system is still visibly and unjustly racialized. Victories within this context can sometimes seem to have mainly symbolic significance. For example, two recent cases, one in the Massachusetts Supreme Judicial Court (2016's *Commonwealth v. Warren*) and another in the Ninth Circuit (2019's *United States v. Brown*), have ruled that police are not entitled to draw an inference about guilt merely because a Black person runs away from them. The recognition that Black Americans have reason to fear the indignity and danger of racially unjust police attention seems meaningful—a consequence of generations of effort on behalf of Black freedom fighters to combine social movement–style street activism with appeals to law. But are those opinions practically significant? Will they lead to less police racial profiling?

These kinds of questions go to the heart of critical race theory, the leading movement in the U.S. legal academy examining race and the law. While there are many ways to interpret its earliest scholarship, the reading that perhaps best captures its origins sees two poles of thought about the relationship between U.S. law and the liberation of subordinated racial groups, each represented by one of the most prominent scholars in its founding generation.

Derrick Bell represents the first pole. Bell, who famously left Harvard Law School over its failure to employ tenured Black women, spent much of the early part of his career litigating school desegregation cases for the NAACP Legal Defense Fund. The popular narrative of that era held that such litigation made substantial headway against the institutions of U.S. racism. Bell's experience led him to a far less sanguine conclusion: despite the movement's legal victories, not much seemed to have changed on the ground. Writing a quarter-century after Brown, he noted that "most black children attend public schools that are both racially isolated and inferior." (Even today, schools remain highly segregated, even without a government act specifically requiring it.) In light of these facts, Bell suggested that pursuing change through the law was destined to come up short. According to his theory of "interest convergence," legal victories for Black Americans can only be won when they are also in the interest of whites. When those interests no longer converge—for example, when school desegregation ceased to be useful in winning a propaganda war with the Soviet Union—any gains will erode.

Patricia Williams represents the second pole of the founding era of critical race theory. Much of her work mounts a defense—complex and nuanced, but a defense nonetheless—of the notion of legal rights. Offering a rejoinder to critical legal studies scholars and Marxists who argued that legal rights reinforced the atomizing tendencies of capitalist liberalism at the expense of a more genuine social solidarity, Williams pointed out that Black Americans had traditionally relied on legal rights–claiming to build a social identity in the first place. In effect, her work identified the white privilege of the legal academic left, even before the term "white privilege" had been coined: it's a lot easier to argue for social solidarity as a substitute for legal rights, Williams argued, when you've always enjoyed social recognition and acknowledged membership. The value of legal rights starts to look very different from the standpoint of Black Americans who have lacked a reserve of social standing to draw on. "While rights may not be ends in themselves," she writes in her 1987 article "Alchemical Notes: Reconstructing Ideals from Deconstructed Rights," "it remains that rights rhetoric has been and continues to be an effective form of discourse for blacks."

> The vocabulary of rights speaks to an establishment that values the guise of stability, and from whom social change for the better must come (whether it is given, taken or smuggled). Change argued for in the sheep's clothing of stability (i.e., "rights") can be effective, even as it destabilizes certain other establishment values (i.e., segregation).

There is an obvious tension between the views of Bell and of Williams. But rather than work out that tension, critical race scholars have traditionally embraced it through the idea of "multiple consciousness." Here is how Mari Matsuda, another prominent early critical race scholar, put it in a 1988 talk, speaking of Black radical activist and philosopher Angela Davis (who was tried but acquitted for murder in the 1970s):

> There are times to stand outside the courtroom door and say "this procedure is a farce, the legal system is corrupt, justice will never prevail in this land as long as privilege rules in the courtroom." There

are times to stand inside the courtroom and say "this is a nation of laws, laws recognizing fundamental values of rights, equality and personhood." Sometimes, as Angela Davis did, there is a need to make both speeches in one day. Is that crazy? Inconsistent? Not to Professor Davis, a Black woman on trial for her life in racist America. It made perfect sense to her, and to the twelve jurors good and true who heard her when she said "your government lies, but *your* law is above such lies."

This ambivalence itself speaks to the liberatory potential of law. Bell's position recognizes that litigation alone cannot achieve social change—a view defended in a different way in Gerald Rosenberg's *The Hollow Hope: Can Courts Bring About Social Change?* (1991). But Williams's position identifies that the law—the ideals it represents, as well as the concrete outcomes that may be instantiated in legislation—can be integrated into political activism by oppressed groups. This is a key insight of the broader field of "law and social movements" as well. We must emphasize that in being capable of invocation on behalf of the subordinated, law still functions as law. That is, it still encapsulates the appeal to fundamental commitments like equal rights, the control of arbitrary power (whether by enslavers or lynch mobs or police), and the principle of treating like cases alike, but it does so as an element of a quest for collective, not individual, empowerment and liberation.

CONTRIBUTORS

Amna A. Akbar is Professor of Law at the Ohio State University Moritz College of Law.

Kate Andrias is Professor of Law at Columbia Law School and a former organizer with the Service Employees International Union.

Sameer Ashar is Clinical Professor of Law and Director of the Workers, Law, and Organizing Clinic at UC Irvine School of Law.

Mary Bernstein is Professor of Sociology at the University of Connecticut and coeditor of *Queer Mobilizations: LGBT Activists Confront the Law.*

Jedediah Britton-Purdy is William S. Beinecke Professor of Law at Columbia Law School and a faculty codirector of the Law and Political Economy Project.

Joseph Fishkin is Professor of Law at UCLA School of Law and coauthor of *The Anti-Oligarchy Constitution*.

William E. Forbath is Lloyd M. Bentsen Chair in Law at UT Austin School of Law and coauthor of *The Anti-Oligarchy Constitution*.

Paul Gowder is Professor of Law at Northwestern University and author *The Rule of Law in the United States: An Unfinished Project of Black Liberation*.

David Singh Grewal is Professor of Law at UC Berkeley School of Law and a faculty codirector of the Law and Political Economy Project.

Amy Kapczynski is Professor of Law at Yale Law School and faculty codirector of the Law and Political Economy Project.

Andrea Scoseria Katz is Associate Professor of Law at Washington University School of Law in St. Louis.

Randall Kennedy is Michael R. Klein Professor of Law at Harvard Law School and author of *Say It Loud! On Race, Law, History, and Culture*.

Zachary Manfredi is the Litigation and Advocacy Director at the Asylum Seeker Advocacy Project.

Sanjukta Paul is Assistant Professor of Law at Wayne State University and author of the forthcoming *Solidarity in the Shadow of Antitrust: Labor and the Legal Idea of Competition.*

Aziz Rana is Richard and Lois Cole Professor of Law at Cornell Law School and author of *The Two Faces of American Freedom.*

Rachel Rebouché is Interim Dean and James E. Beasley Professor of Law at Temple University Beasley School of Law.

Jocelyn Simonson is Professor of Law at Brooklyn Law School and author of a forthcoming book on collective action against the carceral state.

Mark Tushnet is William Nelson Cromwell Professor Emeritus at Harvard Law School and author of *Taking Back the Constitution: Activist Judges and the Next Age of American Law.*